Contents

General Training Module

ACTION PLAN
for IELTS

▸ **Last-minute preparation**

▸ **Practice test**

▸ **Self-study guide**

Vanessa Jakeman
Clare McDowell

CAMBRIDGE
UNIVERSITY PRESS

CAMBRIDGE UNIVERSITY PRESS
Cambridge, New York, Melbourne, Madrid, Cape Town, Singapore, São Paulo, Delhi

Cambridge University Press
The Edinburgh Building, Cambridge CB2 8RU, UK

www.cambridge.org
Information on this title: www.cambridge.org/9780521615310

First published 2006
3rd printing 2008

Printed in the United Kingdom at the University Press, Cambridge

A catalogue record for this publication is available from the British Library

ISBN   978-0-521-615303 Self-study Student's Book (Academic module)
ISBN   978-0-521-615310 Self-study Student's Book (General Training module)
ISBN   978-0-521-61527-3 Self-study Pack (Academic module)
ISBN   978-0-521-61528-0 Self-study Pack (General Training module)
ISBN   978-0-521-615327 cassette (for both modules)
ISBN   978-0-521-615334 CD(audio) (for both modules)

Designed and produced by HL Studios, Long Hanborough

Introduction

Who is *Action Plan for IELTS* for?

Action Plan for IELTS is a short, self-study guide for IELTS, containing one complete practice test. It is designed for students with a limited amount of time to prepare for the IELTS test or for students who have already completed an IELTS course and would like a last-minute guide to the test.

It is for students at intermediate level or above, and is designed for self-study, although it may also be used in class as part of a short preparation course. It shows students what skills are tested in IELTS, what type of questions and tasks they will see, and how to approach them.

There are two editions: one for the Academic module and one for the General Training module. Students should use the appropriate edition for their needs.

How is *Action Plan for IELTS* organised?

Action Plan for IELTS is organised by module: Listening, Reading, Writing and Speaking. These are presented in the same order as the actual test. Each of the four modules begins with a clear introduction, which gives full details of what to expect in that part of the test and what is tested. There is also an overview of the different question types for Listening and Reading, and an explanation of the marking criteria for Writing and Speaking.

Each part of each module gives examples of the Listening and Reading question types, and the Writing and Speaking tasks. The Writing section of the book is organised according to the marking criteria for this module. The criteria are illustrated with short exercises, so students can see exactly what the examiner is looking for and decide how best to approach these parts of the test. The Speaking section of the book provides a step-by-step guide to the three parts of the Speaking test.

The question types and tasks are accompanied by a short, effective *Action Plan*, which gives advice on ways to approach them, and suggests strategies to prepare students for the test. The *Key* includes answers to all the exercises, sample answers to the Writing tasks and, where appropriate, offers tips and strategies that can be used to help get the right answers. An *Audio CD/Cassette* accompanies all listening tasks, and the *Recording Scripts* are also provided.

At the end of the book, there is a complete IELTS *Practice Test*.

How can *Action Plan for IELTS* be used?

Action Plan for IELTS is flexible, and can be used in different ways:

- Students who don't know very much about the test and need a thorough overview should work systematically through the book, and then do the timed Practice Test at the end.
- Students who need more practice in one particular module may prefer to work through the book by doing all the Listening sections first, for example, followed by the Listening sections of the Practice Test, and so on.
- Students who are unsure about particular question types or tasks for the Listening and Reading sections can use the overview with the page references in the introduction for each skill and go directly to that section.

The Listening Test

A 30-minute test of your understanding of spoken English

How many sections does the listening test have?
There are four sections in the listening test. Each section has 10 questions, making a total of 40 questions. The sections become progressively harder. The answers to the questions come in the same order as the information on the recording.

Section 1 (3–4 minutes)
A conversation between two speakers on an everyday, social topic.

Section 2 (3–4 minutes)
A talk by one speaker on a general topic.

Section 3 (3–4 minutes)
A discussion between two to four speakers on a topic related to education.

Section 4 (3–4 minutes)
A lecture or talk by one speaker on an academic or study-related topic.

The whole test lasts about 30 minutes, including the instructions, your reading and listening time, and the time allowed for transferring your answers from the question paper to an answer sheet. The instructions are included on the recording.

ON THE DAY

- The listening test is the first part of the IELTS test.

- Arrive at the test room in plenty of time.

- Take a pencil and rubber with you.

- You write your answers on the question paper as you listen. You can use abbreviations at this stage if you want to.

- You have to transfer your answers to an answer sheet after the test. The recording gives you time to do this.

- You cannot take any books into the test room.

What is the listening test like?

A CD player or overhead sound system is used to play the test. Once the recording has started, you cannot enter or leave the room, or stop or interrupt the test.

There may be a lot of people in the room, so be prepared for this.

You hear the IELTS listening recording only ONCE, so you need to keep up with the questions and make good use of the words on the question paper to help you do this.

Where do I write my final answers?
You transfer your answers carefully from the question paper to an answer sheet at the end of the test.

Will I hear different accents?

Yes, but they will always be clear and easy to understand. You will not hear any grammatical mistakes.

What sort of questions will I get?

There are different question types in the listening test (see pages 8 and 9) and *you can get any mix of question types in any section of the test*. Often you have to choose the correct letter or write up to three words.

Will I get every question type in the test?

No. Each section of the test usually contains two or three question types, so in one complete listening test you could get a maximum of 12 different question types (usually you will get about eight or nine). Sometimes the same question type occurs in more than one section of the test. Remember, you may get a mix of the listening question types in any section of the test.

Why are there different listening situations and question types?

IELTS tests a range of listening skills that you need to live, work or study in an English-speaking environment. This means that you need to be able to understand different types of spoken English in a range of formal and informal contexts.

How can I make best use of the reading time?

You get time to read the questions in each section before you listen. Use this time to work out the topic, underline or highlight key words and decide what sort of information and answers you need to listen for.

What are key words?

Key words carry a lot of information. They are usually words such as nouns or verbs that help you understand the questions.

What general approach should I take to the listening test?

Once the recording begins, use the words on the question paper to help you keep your place. There is an example at the start of the test and the first three sections are divided into two parts to help you follow the conversation, discussion or talk. Write your answers on the question paper as you listen.

How can I improve my score in the listening test?

You can help to improve your score by making sure that you know what each question type tests and by having a general approach for each set of questions. The following pages, divided into four sections, provide you with an **Action Plan** for each set of questions.

What else can I do to prepare for the listening test?

You should listen to spoken English as often as possible, e.g. English-language radio, TV and other forms of media – even music.

How is the listening test marked?

There is one mark per question and this makes a total of 40 marks. Your mark is converted into a Band Score of between 1 and 9. You can get half bands in the listening test, e.g. 6.5.

Is correct spelling important?

Spelling should be correct and handwriting must be clear. Both British and American spellings are acceptable, e.g. *programme/program*, *colour/color*, but you should not use abbreviations. Numbers can be written as words or figures.

Overview of the Listening Question Types

Question type	Action	Key points	Page
Pick from a list	You pick the correct answers from a list of options.	• Write only the correct letters A, B, C, etc. • Answers may be worth one mark or more. • Answers can be written in any order.	10
Form filling	You complete the gaps in the form.	• Write up to three words and/or a number. • Check spelling.	12
Labelling a map or plan	You identify places on the map or plan.	• Write up to three words and/or a number. • If there is a box of answers to choose from, write the correct letter A, B, C, etc.	13
Sentence/ summary completion	You complete the gaps in the sentences or summary.	• Write up to three words and/or a number. • Check spelling. • Check grammar of sentence.	15
Table completion	You complete the table.	• Write up to three words and/or a number. • Check spelling.	17
Short answer questions	You answer the questions.	• Write up to three words and/or a number. • Answers may be worth one mark or more. • Check spelling.	18

Overview of the Listening Question Types

Question type	Action	Key points	Page
Multiple choice	You choose the correct letter A, B or C.	• Write only the correct letters A, B or C.	22
Matching	You match things together, e.g. places and people.	• Write only the correct letters A, B, C, etc. • Options may be used more than once.	23
Labelling a diagram	You label the parts on a diagram.	• Write up to three words and/or a number. • If there is a box of answers to choose from, write the correct letter A, B, C, etc.	24
Note completion	You complete the notes.	• Write up to three words and/or a number.	26
Flow chart completion	You complete the flow chart.	• Write up to three words and/or a number. • If there is a box of answers to choose from, write the correct letter A, B, C, etc.	28
Classification	You decide which category some words belong to.	• Write only the correct letters A, B, C, etc.	29

Listening Section 1

Section 1	Conversation (two speakers)	Social/survival	e.g. booking a hotel
Section 2	Talk by one speaker	General	e.g. radio talk
Section 3	Discussion (two to four speakers)	Educational	e.g. tutorial discussion
Section 4	Talk or lecture by one speaker	Course-related	e.g. university lecture

What is Section 1 like?

You will hear a conversation based on an everyday social/survival situation. Section 1 will help you get used to the listening exercises and test your understanding of simple facts, including names and numbers. There are always two speakers in Section 1. Here is an example of an extract from Section 1.

Hello. I'd like to book a table for four people for tomorrow night, please.

Certainly. Can I have your name and a contact phone number, please?

1 Tick the situations that you think belong to Section 1.

a arranging to meet a friend
b a recorded talk at a museum
c booking a holiday
d negotiating an essay extension
e a discussion on the value of TV
f making a dental appointment
g a lecture on river pollution
h ordering a product

Question Types and Practice Tasks

PICK FROM A LIST

You pick the correct answers from a list of options. There are usually two or three answers to pick from about six options. The options are labelled A, B, C, etc.

What does pick from a list test?

You have to pick out the correct facts from the recording and match these to words in the options. You may not hear the exact words that you read in the options, so you will be listening for a word or words with a similar meaning.

2 Match the words or phrases in Box A with words or phrases of a similar meaning in Box B.

A
identification   study English
fly   building   painting
headgear   vehicle   meal
bag   thunderstorm
winter sports

B
helmet   suitcase   passport
car   house   wet weather
learn a language
go by plane   lunch
skiing   picture

How should I write my answers?

You only need to write the correct letters (A, B, C, etc.) on an answer sheet. You can write these in any order. Sometimes a question is worth one mark (for finding all the answers) and sometimes the question has one mark for each answer. This affects how you write your answers on the answer sheet.

ACTION PLAN

▸ Read the question carefully and note how many options you must pick.
▸ Underline or highlight the key words in the main question.
▸ Read the list of options and underline or highlight any key words.
▸ Re-phrase these options in your own words (if possible).
▸ As you listen, choose the correct answers.

NOW TRY THE TASK

Read the telephone conversation in the speech bubbles below and answer the questions.

Is that the Sydney Motor Registry? I'd like some information about taking a driving test. Do I need my own car, for instance?

Not necessarily. But first you must pass the knowledge test, that's the test of the road rules. That's done on a computer... here at this office. And you'll need to book for that. And then you can take the actual road driving test. That can be in your car or the driving school's car if you take lessons. And, of course, you must be at least 18 years old.

Note that this question is worth two marks because you have to understand quite a long conversation to get both answers.

Questions 3–4

*Choose **TWO** letters **A–E**.*

• *Which **TWO** things must the girl do before she can take the road driving test?*

    A have her own car
    B have her own computer
    C pass the road rules test
    D book driving lessons
    E reach the age of 18

FORM FILLING

You complete the gaps in the form using up to three words and/or a number. Some of the information may already be completed to help you.

What does form filling test?

Like all completion tasks, form filling tests your ability to predict what is missing in the gaps. You need to listen for important details like names, dates, places, times, etc. Sometimes these are spelt out. If they are not, you still need to try to spell the answers correctly. Make sure you can match spoken numbers to written numbers.

5 Say these times in two different ways, e.g. *two ten / ten past two in the afternoon*.

   2.10 pm   7.50 am   6.45 am   10.15 am   1.00 am   13.00 hrs

6 Say these dates in two different ways, e.g. *the first of February / February the first*.

   1st February   21st November   24 March   December 22nd   August 18

7 Look at the form below and decide what type of information you would need to listen for. Make a note in the column on the right.

Casualty Department	Patient's admission details	Type of information
Family name	*Mitchell*	*a name*
Given name	....	a ....
Address	*26 Lake Street, Newport*	*an address*
Date of birth	....	b ....
Name of doctor	....	c ....
Reason for admission	....	d ....

How should I write my answers?

Write the correct words and/or numbers on the answer sheet. Use no more words than you are told to use and make sure you spell them correctly. You can write numbers in words or figures.

ACTION PLAN

▸ Read the instructions carefully to see how many words you can write.
▸ Look at the form and the information and decide what it is about.
▸ Note the order of the questions.
▸ Look at the gaps and any headings and decide what type of information is required.
▸ Underline or highlight the key words around each gap and use these to help you listen for the answer.
▸ As you listen, complete the form.

NOW TRY THE TASK

Listen to Extract 1. (CD Track 1)

Questions 8–11

Complete the form below.
Write **NO MORE THAN THREE WORDS AND/OR A NUMBER** *for each answer.*

Motor Registry — Telephone messages		
Caller's name	8	....
Date of birth	9	....
Telephone	10	0412..................
Type of car	11	....

RECORDING SCRIPT PAGE 111

LABELLING A MAP OR PLAN

You identify places on the map or plan, using words and/or a number from a box of options. The parts to be labelled will have an arrow and the question number beside them.

Alternatively, places may already be identified on the map with letters. You match these letters to the information in the numbered questions.

What does labelling a map or plan test?
This type of question tests your ability to understand words and expressions of place and location. You must answer with information from the recording.

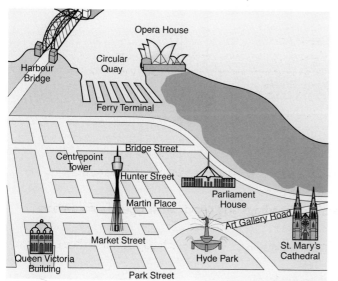

To practise using a map, look at the picture and answer the questions.

12 What is the building in the bottom left-hand corner?

13 Where on the map is St. Mary's Cathedral?

14 Name two streets that are parallel to Park Street.

15 What structure is at the top of the map in the middle?

How should I write my answers?
If you have a box of options, you only need to write the correct letter A, B, C, etc. Otherwise you write the words you hear on the recording. Only use the number of words you are told to use and remember to spell them correctly.

ACTION PLAN

▸ Look at the map or plan to form a general idea of the content.
▸ Look at the parts of the map or plan you need to label and decide what kinds of words are needed.
▸ Use the words already provided in the map or plan to guide your listening.
▸ When you listen, pay particular attention to expressions of location such as *in the middle, on the corner, next to, above/below, straight ahead*, etc. as the answer may depend on your understanding these words.
▸ As you listen, choose the correct answers.

NOW TRY THE TASK

((◀ *Listen to Extract 2. (CD Track 2)*

Questions 16–19

Label the street plan below.
*Write **NO MORE THAN THREE** words for each answer.*

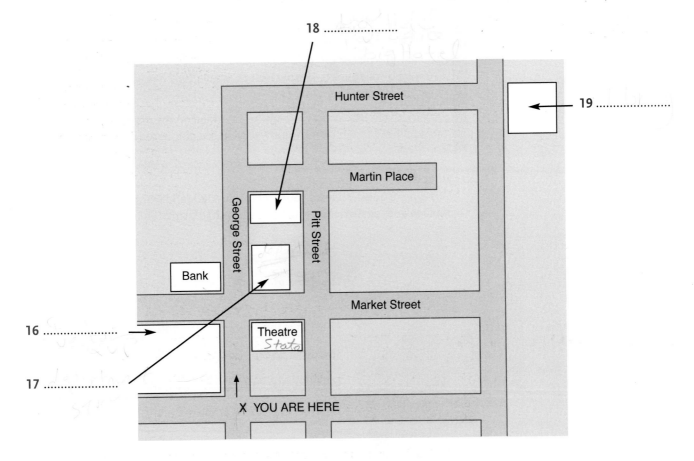

RECORDING SCRIPT PAGE 111
ANSWERS PAGE 103
PRACTICE TEST PAGE 88

Listening Section 2

Section 1	Conversation (two speakers)	Social/survival	e.g. booking a hotel
Section 2	**Talk by one speaker**	**General**	**e.g. radio talk**
Section 3	Discussion (two to four speakers)	Educational	e.g. tutorial discussion
Section 4	Talk or lecture by one speaker	Course-related	e.g. university lecture

What is Section 2 like?

You will hear a talk by one speaker on a topic of general interest. Section 2 is a little harder than Section 1. You will have to decide what the important details or facts on the recording are, without the help of another speaker's questions to guide you.

1 Read these short talks. Decide where or when you might hear them. Pick out the important details in each one and complete the box below.

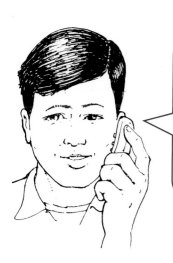

A

Welcome to Brighton Pavilion. You can pause this commentary at any time by pressing the red pause button. The Pavilion was initially built in 1784 and then re-built between 1815 and 1820 for the Prince Regent, who loved travelling. To celebrate this, he chose a mix of Indian and Chinese architectural styles for his palace, as you can see as you walk around.

B

Koala bears are one of the most popular animals with visitors to our zoo because of their loveable appearance. However, a word of caution! They aren't always as nice as they look and they will happily use their long claws to protect themselves if they fear attack. So do take care.

> **A** *Recorded audio tour* / ....
>
> **B** ....

Question Types and Practice Tasks

▶▶▶▶▶▶▶▶▶▶▶▶▶▶▶▶▶▶▶▶▶

SENTENCE/SUMMARY COMPLETION

You complete the sentences or summary by writing up to three words and/or a number in the gaps. The gaps can come at the beginning, in the middle or at the end of the sentence.

What is the difference between sentence and summary completion?
In the listening test, there is very little difference. Sentences are joined together to form a summary. Follow the **Action Plan** for sentence completion, remembering that sentences always have a main verb and a subject, and articles and prepositions are important and can be a useful guide to missing words.

2 Decide what type of information is needed to complete the sentences below. Is it a word, e.g. a noun, an adjective, a verb? Is it a number, e.g. a time, a measurement, an age?

Type of word(s)

Lectures begin at .... in the morning.   *a number (time)*

  a .... can carry up to 350 passengers.
  b .... are in danger of becoming extinct.
  c The Rosetta Stone was discovered in Egypt in ....
  d The tower is made of ....
  e Aboriginal art is extremely .... these days.
  f Research shows that cigarette smoking is ....

How should I write my answers?

If you have a box of options, you only need to write the correct answer A, B, C, etc. Otherwise you write the words you hear on the recording. Use no more words than you are told to use and make sure you spell them correctly. You can write numbers in words or figures.

ACTION PLAN

▶ Read the instructions carefully to see how many words you can write in your answer.
▶ Underline or highlight the key words in each question.
▶ Note the position of the gaps in the sentences.
▶ Decide what kind of information is needed to complete the sentences, e.g. a noun, a number, a verb or an adjective.
▶ Note any grammatical words in the questions, such as articles or prepositions, which can help you get the correct answer.
▶ Underline or highlight the key words around each gap and use these to listen for the answer.
▶ As you listen, complete the sentences or summary.

NOW TRY THE TASK

(((▶ *Listen to Extract 1. (CD Track 3)*

Questions 3–6

Complete the sentences below.
*Write **NO MORE THAN THREE WORDS AND/OR A NUMBER** for each answer.*

3 The Bell Rock lighthouse was built almost .... ago.
4 The tower is made of ....
5 The reef is dangerous to ships because it is ....
6 Initial construction took place during the ....

7 How did you write the answer to question 3?

RECORDING SCRIPT PAGE 111

TABLE COMPLETION

You complete the table by writing up to three words and/or a number in the gaps provided. Some of the information may already be completed to help you.

How does table completion differ from sentence/summary completion?
In table completion you only have to fill in the gaps in the columns. There are no complete sentences.

8 Look at the table below. What is it about? What are the key words?
9 What kind of information is missing for hotels A, B and C?

	Rate per night	Rate includes	Hotel facilities
Hotel A	$75		TV in room
Hotel B			Swimming pool
Hotel C	$220	Full breakfast	

How should I write my answers?
Write the correct words and/or numbers on the answer sheet. Use no more words than you are told to use and make sure you spell them correctly. You can write numbers in words or figures.

ACTION PLAN

▶ Read the instructions carefully to see how many words you can write in your answer.
▶ Look at the table and the information included and decide what it is about.
▶ Look at the gaps and headings and decide what type of information is required.
▶ Note the order of the questions.
▶ Underline or highlight the key words around each gap and use these to listen for the answer.
▶ As you listen, complete the table.

NOW TRY THE TASK

((▶ *Listen to Extract 2. (CD Track 4)*

Questions 10–12

Complete the table below.
Write **NO MORE THAN THREE WORDS AND/OR A NUMBER** *for each answer.*

Cinema	Film	Times showing	Type of film
One	*Shrek 2*	**10**	animation
Two	**11**	6.15 pm	documentary
Three	*Armour of God*	5.30 / 9.15 pm	**12** ....

RECORDING SCRIPT PAGE 111

SHORT ANSWER QUESTIONS

You answer the questions using up to three words and/or a number.

What is involved in short answer questions?

There are two types of short answer question. Type 1 is where you answer an actual question, and Type 2 is where you make a list of up to three things. You need to underline or highlight the key words in the question that tell you what kind of information to listen out for. *Wh-* question words are often key words in Type 1 questions.

| **Where?** *place* | **Which?** *thing* | **When?** *time* | **What?** *thing* |
| **Why?** *reason* | **Who?** *person* | **How?** *method/manner/way* | |

13 Underline or highlight the *Wh-* question words and the other key words in these questions and say what kind of answer they require.

Type of information

Which street is the bookshop situated in? — *name of street*

When is Sarah going to the restaurant? — **a** ....

Where can you see paintings by Van Gogh? — **b** ....

How many people were at the concert? — **c** ....

Why did Rudi telephone his mother? — **d** ....

What did the Customs Officer find in the man's bag? — **e** ....

Who came to the party? — **f** ....

What happened to the old lady? — **g** ....

How did the student hurt his foot? — **h** ....

How are Type 2 questions marked?

In this type of short answer question, you will have to make a list of up to three things. Note the question numbers as this will tell you how many marks they are worth.

Look at these example questions to see how many marks each one is worth.

> *Question 17*
> *Name* **TWO** *places where you can see paintings by Van Gogh.*

There is only one question, so you need both answers for one mark.

> *Questions 18–20*
> *Name* **THREE** *things that the Customs Officer found in the man's bag.*

There are three questions, so you get one mark for each answer.

How should I write my answers?

Write the correct words and/or numbers on the answer sheet. Use no more words than you are told to use and make sure you spell them correctly. You can write numbers in words or figures.

ACTION PLAN

▶ Check the instructions to see how many words you can write in your answer.
▶ Check to see if all the questions follow the same format.
▶ Underline or highlight the key words in each question and decide what kind of information you need to listen out for.
▶ As you listen, write your answers.

NOW TRY THE TASK

((▶ *Listen to Extract 3. (CD Track 5)*

Answer the questions below.

Write **NO MORE THAN THREE WORDS** *for each answer.*

Questions 14 and 15

14 On which level is the new section located?   ....

15 What does the Gallery exhibit besides paintings?   ....

Question 16

16 Name **TWO** things which accompany
   the special exhibitions.   ....
   ....

17 How does question 16 differ from questions 14 and 15?

RECORDING SCRIPT PAGE 111
ANSWERS PAGE 103
PRACTICE TEST PAGE 89

Listening Section 3

Section 1	Conversation (two speakers)	Social/survival	e.g. booking a hotel
Section 2	Talk by one speaker	General	e.g. radio talk
Section 3	**Discussion (two to four speakers)**	**Educational**	**e.g. tutorial discussion**
Section 4	Talk or lecture by one speaker	Course-related	e.g. university lecture

These are the Question Types you will practise here
MULTIPLE CHOICE
MATCHING
LABELLING A DIAGRAM

What is Section 3 like?
You will hear a discussion with up to four speakers on an educational topic. Section 3 is more difficult than Sections 1 and 2. You will have to follow the discussion and listen for important facts, reasons or ideas. You may also have to identify views or opinions.

How can I follow the discussion?
1 Look at part of a discussion with three speakers. What is the logical order for them to speak in?

(A) *Is it that old? I hadn't realised that.*

(C) *No. A lot of people don't realise that, but I still think ancient Egyptian art is more interesting than rock art.*

(B) *Much Australian Aboriginal rock art is more than 40,000 years old; that's five times older than the Egyptian pyramids.*

2 Now look at this discussion with three speakers, one of whom speaks twice. What order should they speak in?

(A) *Aren't there two main types of tea: green and black?*

(B) *I believe it comes from the dried leaves of a small tree called a camellia bush. It's mostly grown in sub-tropical areas like Sri Lanka, Japan and China.*

(C) *Where do we get tea from?*

(D) *Yes. You're right. Green tea is picked and dried quickly, which is what gives it a mild flavour. That's why it's very popular in China and Japan.*

3 Do any of the speakers in either discussion give a personal opinion?

4 Which of the speakers in either discussion state a fact or give a reason?

How can I pick out important facts, ideas or reasons?
You need to listen to what the speakers ask or tell each other, and then decide what their main point is. Sometimes you have to understand how the idea has been re-worded in the questions.

5 Read the following exchanges A and B, and choose the correct sentence endings from the boxes.

A **Student**
Are there any areas of my work that you think I could improve?

Tutor *Well, your work's been pretty good this term. I like the way you set out your data. You could perhaps learn a bit more about the topic, that's the only thing. But you obviously pay attention in lectures.*

The student needs to work on his
i concentration.
ii presentation skills.
iii subject knowledge.

B **Student**
Oh hi, I can't find Mr Peterson. Is he on holiday?

Administrator *Actually he's just back from two weeks' study leave but he's not here today. He seems to have developed a nasty cold. Try joining his four o'clock class tomorrow. He should be back by then.*

Mr Peterson is unavailable because he is
i off sick.
ii on study leave.
iii teaching another class.

6 Read the following exchanges A, B and C, and decide whether the speakers agree with each other or not.

A *A camel's hump contains water so that it can go without drinking for many days, doesn't it?*

I'm not so sure. I think it's made of fat, which can be converted to energy and water. But I don't think it actually contains water.

B *It's awful when people throw rubbish and cigarette butts in the street and just expect someone else to clean it up. It's really so lazy!*

You have a point. It is lazy of them. But if we had more public rubbish bins, that might help too.

C *If you want to lose weight, you should cut out fats and carbohydrates; things like potatoes, rice, pasta... and just eat meat and vegetables.*

That's all very well but it's not very healthy. You need carbohydrates to give you energy. Personally, I think it's better to try to have a balanced diet.

Question Types and Practice Tasks

MULTIPLE CHOICE
You choose the correct answer to a question from three options (A, B or C).

What is multiple choice?
There are two types of multiple choice questions, and you can get both types together in the same set of questions.

A question followed by three possible options.

How was the project funded?	The project was funded by
A by the government	**A** the government.
B by the university	**B** the university.
C by raising money	**C** raising money.

An unfinished statement followed by three possible endings.

How should I write my answers?
You only need to write the correct letter A, B or C on the answer sheet.

ACTION PLAN

▸ Read what is given carefully and note whether it is a question or a statement.
▸ Underline or highlight the key words.
▸ Re-phrase the question or statement in your own words.
▸ Read the three possible answers and underline or highlight the key words.
▸ Try to re-phrase the possible answers in your own words.
▸ As you listen, choose the correct answer.

NOW TRY THE TASK

((◉ *Listen to Extract 1. (CD Track 6)*

Question 7

*Choose the correct letter **A**, **B** or **C**.*

7 Why do flamingos in captivity need
   to eat algae?
   A to ensure they remain healthy
   B to supplement their diet
   C to keep their bodies pink

8 How did you re-phrase the three options?

9 Can you explain why two of the options are not correct?

RECORDING SCRIPT PAGE 112

MATCHING

You answer the questions by matching the words in the list (1, 2, 3, etc.) to the correct word or phrase in the box (A, B, C, etc.). There may not be a match for every item in the box, and you may need to use some items in the box more than once.

What is matching?

You will see a list of numbered questions and a list of options labelled with a letter. You match the correct option to each question based on what you hear.

A requires stamina	*takes a lot of energy*
B played worldwide	....
C potentially dangerous	....
D extremely popular	....
E expensive equipment	....
F easy to learn	....
G exciting to watch	....

10 Look at the list of options A–G and re-write the phrases in your own words. Describe each sport (1–5) using some of your alternative expressions.

1 table tennis
2 cycling
3 snowboarding
4 basketball
5 football

How should I write my answers?

You only need to write the correct letters A, B, C, etc. on the answer sheet.

ACTION PLAN

▶ Look at the list of numbered questions and decide what they have in common.
▶ Say them quietly to yourself to help you recognise them on the recording.
▶ Read the list of options, noting any heading in the box.
▶ Re-phrase each of the options in your own words.
▶ As you listen, match the options to the questions.

NOW TRY THE TASK

Questions 11–14

What does the lecturer say about each student?
*Choose FOUR answers from the box and write the correct letters **A–G** next to questions 11–14.*

> *David's work was good but lacked content. The paper would be better if it included some more examples but there's no need for him to re-submit.*

> *Lee's research is groundbreaking and of a very high standard. I don't have any concerns about him.*

> *Rosa's work is usually pretty good, though certainly not brilliant. She deserves a solid pass.*

> *Kim's work hasn't been assessed yet, so I'm not in a position to comment.*

Comments on students' work
A needs to re-submit
B reasonable level throughout
C still to be marked
D shows potential
E needs more data
F excellent original work
G below average

11 David .... 13 Lee ....
12 Rosa .... 14 Kim ....

15 Underline or highlight the words in the speech bubbles that match the answers for this task.

LABELLING A DIAGRAM

You label the parts on a diagram using up to three words and/or a number. The parts to be labelled will have an arrow and the question number beside them. You may have a box of possible answers to choose from.

What sort of diagram will I have to label?
You may have a diagram illustrating a process or you may have to label parts of an object. The parts to be labelled will be clearly indicated.

How should I write my answers?
If you have a box of options, you only need to write the correct answer A, B, C, etc. Otherwise you write the words you hear on the recording. Only use the number of words you are told to use and remember to spell them correctly.

ACTION PLAN

▶ Read the instructions to see how many words you can write in your answer.
▶ Look carefully at the diagram and decide what it is about.
▶ Note any title or labels already included.
▶ If you have a box of possible answers, read the words in the box and think about how they relate to the diagram.
▶ Think about where the labels might go or what the unlabelled parts might be.
▶ As you listen, choose an answer from the box or the recording.

NOW TRY THE TASK

((◀ *Listen to Extract 2. (CD Track 7)*

Questions 16–18

Label the diagram below.
*Choose three answers from the box and write the correct letters **A–G** next to questions 16–18.*

A metal frame
B wing
C plastic cells
D door
E computer
F road map
G camera

16 ....

17 ....

18 ....

Prototype for a plastic car

multi-directional wheels

RECORDING SCRIPT PAGE 112
ANSWERS PAGE 103
PRACTICE TEST PAGE 90

Listening Section 4

Section 1	Conversation (two speakers)	Social/survival	e.g. booking a hotel
Section 2	Talk by one speaker	General	e.g. radio talk
Section 3	Discussion (two to four speakers)	Educational	e.g. tutorial discussion
Section 4	**Talk or lecture by one speaker**	**Course-related**	**e.g. university lecture**

What is Section 4 like?
You will hear a lecture or talk based on a course-related topic. Section 4 is the hardest section of the test. The question types are similar to those in Sections 1–3, but you will have to follow the development of the lecture and identify the main ideas or key points.

How is a lecture usually structured?
The language is quite formal. The speaker usually begins by telling the listeners what he or she is going to say and then the main points are clearly identified, often illustrated with examples.

Today, I'm going to talk about the role of computers in early education. Firstly we'll look at keyboard skills and young children.

How can I follow the lecture and predict what I might hear?
Look carefully at the vocabulary in the questions and listen out for 'signpost' words used during the talk, e.g. *firstly, on the other hand, one way is*, as these will help you predict what the speaker is going to say. The words given will help you predict what is coming.

1 Look at the signpost words 1–10, which signal different kinds of information. Match the words in the box with the meanings a–j.

1 One way...
2 In fact...
3 And... in addition
4 Surprisingly enough...
5 By contrast...
6 Lastly...
7 Let's move on to...
8 Generally speaking,...
9 In other words,...
10 On the other hand,...

a another example
b something that is unexpected
c making the point clearer by giving supporting information
d something quite different / the opposite
e a closing statement or final point in a list
f a possible action that can produce the result you want
g a change of subject
h most of the time, usually
i providing an opposing point of view
j re-stating something in a different way

A Not many people actually voted at the last election. ...., the figures indicated that less than half of the eligible voters turned out on the day.

2 Complete the speech bubbles A–F with the most appropriate signpost words from the box on page 25. There may be more than one possibility.

B Some people argue that exercise is the key to good health. ...., if you don't take exercise, you don't run the risk of injuring yourself!

C Basically there are two approaches to writing. .... is to make some notes before you begin, and the other is to dive in without a plan. But for academic writing, we definitely recommend the first.

D We've been through all the main points, so ...., I'd like to wish you all good luck with the exam.

E There are various views on the causes of pollution, but ...., it is felt that burning fossil fuels is mostly to blame.

F You'd think that learning a foreign alphabet would be difficult but ...., it's not so hard once you get started.

Question Types and Practice Tasks

▶▶▶▶▶▶▶▶▶▶▶▶▶▶▶▶▶▶

NOTE COMPLETION
You complete the notes by writing no more than three words and/or a number in the gap. Some of the information may already be completed to help you.

What does note completion involve?
You complete the notes with the words you hear on the recording. Notes may not follow standard grammatical rules or layout, e.g. there may be articles or auxiliary verbs missing, or the notes may be lists with bullet points.

How can I tell where the answers are in the recording?
The words included in the task can guide you through the recording, so it is important to read all the notes in the task carefully during your reading time.

3 Read through the set of notes below and decide what the topic is. Use your own words to form a question for each gap.

4 Work out what type of information is needed to complete the notes below, e.g. *an object, a number,* etc.

((◗ *Listen to Extract 1 (CD Track 8) and check your predictions with the recording script on page 112.*

String of human DNA
- approximately three feet long
- looks like a (5) ....
- includes between 50,000 and 100,000 genes

Complete set known as the human genome
Is very similar to many (6) .... and ....

How should I write my answers?

Write the correct words and/or numbers on the answer sheet. Use no more words than you are told to use and make sure you spell them correctly. You can write numbers in words or figures.

ACTION PLAN

▶ Read the instructions carefully to see how many words you can write.
▶ Look at the layout of the task, e.g. bullet points or continuous notes.
▶ Read the notes and decide what the topic is.
▶ Try to re-phrase the notes to form a question in your own words for each gap.
▶ Underline or highlight the key words around each gap and use these to help you listen for the answer.
▶ Note whether there is more than one gap for any of the questions.
▶ As you listen, complete the notes.

NOW TRY THE TASK

((◖ *Listen to Extract 2. (CD Track 9)*

Questions 7–9

Complete the notes below.

Write **NO MORE THAN THREE WORDS** *for each answer.*

Lonely Planet

– head office located in (7) .... but branches worldwide

– uses a variety of (8) .... to be competitive
  e.g. – tracking customers
     – allowing name to be used by a (9) ....

RECORDING SCRIPT PAGE 112

FLOW CHART COMPLETION

A flow chart always represents a sequence of events or a process. You complete the flow chart by writing up to three words and/or a number in the gaps. You may have a box of possible answers to choose from.

What is flow chart completion?
Flow chart completion is like note completion. It may not follow standard grammatical rules or layout.

How should I write my answers?
Write the correct words and/or numbers on the answer sheet. Use no more words than you are told to use and make sure you spell them correctly. You can write numbers in words or figures.

ACTION PLAN

▶ Look carefully at the questions and decide what the overall topic is.
▶ Note how the sequence works.
▶ Decide what type of word is needed to fill the gaps, e.g. a noun or a verb.
▶ As you listen, complete the flow chart.

NOW TRY THE TASK

((◖ *Listen to Extract 3. (CD Track 10)*

Questions 10–13
Complete the flow chart below.
*Write **NO MORE THAN THREE WORDS** for each answer.*

Olive oil production

Olives picked (**10**) ....

↓

Fruit taken to the (**11**) .... and crushed

↓

Extra virgin oil produced from first pressing

↓

Product bottled and (**12**) ....

↓

Transported to markets (**13**) .... and ....

Signpost words
• after this initial process
• then
• finally
• the first step is to
• incidentally

14 Look at the box of signpost words and put them in the order that best fits the information in the flow chart above, then listen to Extract 3 again.

RECORDING SCRIPT PAGE 112

CLASSIFICATION

You decide which category some words or statements belong to. The categories are usually A, B, C, etc. The words or statements are usually the questions.

What does classification involve?

A classification task has a list of options labelled A, B, C, etc. Based on what you hear, you match the words or ideas in the questions to one of the options.

15 Look at the example below and decide what the topic is. Read the question and note how it relates to the numbered items and options A–C.

Which method works best for the following materials?

A burying	1 aluminium ....
B burning	2 glass ....
C recycling	3 plastics ....
	4 paper ....
	5 green waste ....

16 What do the words A–C refer to?

How should I write my answers?

You only need to write the correct letter A, B, C, etc. on the answer sheet.

ACTION PLAN

▶ Look at the task and decide what the topic is.
▶ Look at the main question and the numbered items that follow it.
▶ Look at the numbered items and decide what they have in common.
▶ Look at the words A, B, C, etc. and decide how they relate to the question.
▶ As you listen, decide which letter best fits each numbered item.

NOW TRY THE TASK

((◖ *Listen to Extract 4. (CD Track 11)*

Questions 17–21

According to the speaker, which method works best for mastering these skills?

*Write the correct letters **A–C** next to questions 17–21.*

A language laboratory	17 speaking ....
B self-study	18 listening ....
C small group work	19 pronunciation ....
	20 grammar ....
	21 reading ....

RECORDING SCRIPT PAGE 112
ANSWERS PAGE 104
PRACTICE TEST PAGE 91

The General Training Reading Test

A 60-minute test of your reading skills

How many sections does the reading test have?
There are three sections in the reading test. In each section there are 13 or 14 questions. There are 40 questions in total. The number of reading passages in each section varies: in Section 1 you may get up to three short passages, in Section 2 you will get two passages, and in Section 3 there is one long passage. The whole test lasts an hour and altogether, you have to read a maximum of 2350 words.

What is the reading test like?
You will receive a reading test booklet with the passages and questions in it, and an answer sheet.

Where do I write my answers?

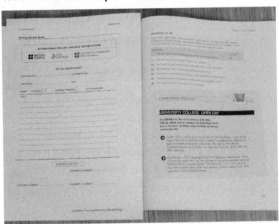

You can write on the question booklet but you must write all your final answers on the reading answer sheet.

What are the passages about?

Section 1	Up to three short passages related to everyday life, e.g. theatre brochures, accommodation lists, transport information, etc.
Section 2	Two passages related to education and training or work, e.g. college brochures, course information, manuals, etc.
Section 3	One long passage on a topic of general interest, e.g. newspaper/magazine articles, book extracts or internet texts on the environment, business, people, transport, weather, etc.

Will I be able to understand the passages?
Although the topics may seem unfamiliar to you, none of the passages will contain technical information or specialist vocabulary that is not explained. Sometimes, however, you will need to ignore unknown words or guess their meanings.

What sort of questions will I get?
There are many different question types in the reading test (see pages 32–3). Often you have to choose the correct letter or write some words. If you have to write an answer, you will never have to use more than three words and/or a number.

☐ ON THE DAY

- The reading test is the second part of the IELTS test, held after the listening test on the same day.

- The supervisor will write the start and finish times on the board, and give you a ten-minute warning before the end.

- You must write your answers in pencil on the answer sheet.

- Unlike the listening test, there is no transfer time. After one hour, the test is over and you must hand in the answer sheet.

Will I get every question type in the test?

No. Each section of the test usually contains two to four question types, so in one complete reading test you could get a maximum of 12 different question types (usually you will get about eight or nine). Sometimes the same question type occurs in more than one section of the test. *Remember, you may get a mix of the reading question types in any section of the test.*

Why are there different reading question types?

IELTS tests a range of reading skills that you need for survival and study purposes. For example, if a passage is about eight different courses, then you may be expected to match short descriptions to these courses. This shows whether or not you can identify the individual features of the courses. If a passage contains a lot of detailed information, you may get sentence completion questions that ask you to find specific information.

These are the main skills that IELTS tests:
• reading quickly to get a general idea or find a particular word
• finding detailed or factual information
• understanding themes and main ideas
• identifying views and claims
• identifying the overall theme of the passage.

What general approach should I take to the reading test?

Do the sections in the order in which they come. Always read the title and sub-heading (if there is one) of each passage and use these to form an idea of what the passage is about. Then read quickly through the questions and note what type they are. Read the passage(s) quickly before you start doing the questions to see how the topic is developed and note the main ideas. Start with the first set of questions.

How can I improve my score in the reading test?

You can help to improve your score by making sure that you know what each question type tests and by having a general approach for each set of questions. The following pages, divided into three sections, provide you with an **Action Plan** for each set of questions.

What else can I do to prepare for the reading test?

You should read as widely as you can and practise reading quickly to get the main ideas. You should also familiarise yourself with different types of text, such as newspaper articles, course information, college brochures, manuals, magazine articles and information on the internet.

How is the reading test marked?

There is one mark per question and this makes a total of 40 marks. Your mark is converted into a Band Score of between 1 and 9. You can get half bands in the reading test, e.g. 6.5.

Is correct spelling important?

Your spelling must be correct and your handwriting must be clear. The answers must come from the reading passages, and you will lose marks if you copy words incorrectly. You should not use abbreviations unless they are in the passage, and you should check plurals.

Overview of the General Training Reading Question Types

Question type	Action	Key points	Page
Short answer questions	You answer the questions using words from the passage.	• Answers are in passage order. • Write up to three words and/or a number. • Check spelling with passage. • Don't include any unnecessary words.	34
True / False / Not Given	You decide whether the statement agrees with or contradicts the passage, or whether there is no information.	• Answers are in passage order. • Write True, False or Not Given.	36
Sentence completion	You complete the gaps in the sentences using words from the passage.	• Answers are in passage order. • Write up to three words and/or a number. • Check spelling with passage. • Check grammar of completed sentence. • Don't include any unnecessary words.	37
Notes / table / flow chart completion	You complete the gaps in the notes, table or flow chart using words from the passage.	• Answers may not be in passage order. • Write up to three words and/or a number. • Check spelling with passage. • Don't include any unnecessary words.	38
Labelling a diagram	You name parts of a diagram using words from the passage.	• Answers may not be in passage order. • Write up to three words and/or a number. • Check spelling with passage. • Don't include any unnecessary words. • Mark relevant parts of passage while reading.	39
Paragraph headings	You choose the correct heading for each paragraph from a list of headings.	• Underline or highlight main ideas in paragraphs. • Write the correct number i, ii, iii, etc. • Some headings will not be used.	41
Finding information in paragraphs	You find the paragraph that contains the information in the question.	• Write A, B, C, etc. • Some letters may be used more than once. • Some paragraphs may not be tested.	43

Overview of the General Training Reading Question Types

Question type	Action	Key points	Page
Matching	You match statements to items in a box.	• Statements are not in passage order. • Boxed items are usually in passage order. • Write A, B, C, etc. • Some letters may be used more than once. • Some letters may not be used.	44
Classification	You decide which category some statements or features belong to.	• Answers are not in passage order. • Write A, B, C, etc. • Some letters may be used more than once. • Some letters may not be used.	45
Multiple choice	You choose the correct letter A, B, C or D.	• Answers are in passage order. • Write A, B, C or D. • Check other options are wrong.	47
Pick from a list	You pick the correct answers from a list of options.	• Answers may not be in passage order. • Write A, B, C, etc. • Each answer may score one mark or the whole question may score one mark.	48
Yes / No / Not Given	You decide whether the statement agrees with or contradicts the writer's views or claims, or whether there is no information.	• Answers are in passage order. • Write Yes, No or Not Given.	49
Sentence completion with a box	You complete the sentences by selecting the correct ending from a box of options.	• Answers are in passage order. • Write A, B, C, etc. • Some letters may not be used. • Check grammar and meaning of sentence.	51
Summary completion	You complete the gaps in the summary using words from the passage.	• Answers may not be in passage order. • Write up to three words and/or a number. • Check spelling with passage. • Check grammar of completed summary. • Don't include any unnecessary words.	53
Summary completion with a box	You complete the gaps in the summary using words or phrases from a box.	• Answers may not be in passage order. • Write A, B, C, etc. • Some letters will not be used. • Check spelling with passage. • Check grammar of completed summary.	55

General Training Reading Section 1

Section 1	13–14 questions	Up to three short passages	Total 600 words maximum
Section 2	13–14 questions	Two passages	Total 750 words maximum
Section 3	13–14 questions	One long passage	Total 1000 words maximum

What are the Section 1 passages about?

Section 1 passages are all related to everyday life in an English-speaking country. They come from newspapers, leaflets, advertising messages, instructions and other documents that provide information. They may be in the form of a contents list, a short paragraph, a set of instructions, advertisements, etc.

Question Types and Practice Tasks

SHORT ANSWER QUESTIONS

You answer the questions using up to three words and/or a number from the passage. The answers in the passage are in the same order as the questions.

What is involved in short answer questions?

You need to underline or highlight the key words in the questions that tell you what kind of information to find. These are often words like *when*, *what*, *how many*, *which*, etc.

Here is an example of key words in a question:
<u>What skills</u> do you need to join the course for <u>general technicians</u>?

How should I write my answers?

You should only use words from the passage, and you must use no more words than you are told to use. They should be written exactly as they are in the reading passage (numbers too) and they have to be spelt correctly. Do not include unnecessary words, or repeat words that are already provided in the sentence.

ACTION PLAN

▶ Read the instructions carefully to see how many words you can write.
▶ Underline or highlight the key words in each question and decide what kind of information you need to look for.
▶ Start with the first question and read the passage quickly to see if you can find words that are the same as the key words or have a similar meaning.
▶ Read around these words to find the answer.
▶ Decide exactly which words and/or numbers you should write as the answer.

NOW TRY THE TASK

Read the library advertisement and answer the questions below.
*Choose **NO MORE THAN TWO WORDS AND/OR A NUMBER** from the*
reading passage for each answer.

Hove Library

182-186 Church Road

Hove

BN3 2EG

Tel (01273) 290700
Fax (01273) 296931

Reference library	(01273) 296942
Music library	(01273) 296941
Computer bookings	(01273) 296939
Joining the library	(01273) 290700
Book renewals	(01273) 296939

Opening hours

Monday	10.00 am–2 pm
Tuesday	9.30 am–7.30 pm
Wednesday	9.30 am–5.30 pm
Thursday	9.30 am–5.30 pm
Friday	9.30 am–5.30 pm
Saturday	9.30 am–5 pm

Parking is available outside the building for disabled drivers at no charge.
All other drivers should use the pay and display parking in the local area.

Key words	Information	Answer
1 In which town is the library?	*a place*	
2 What is the postcode for the library?		
3 What number do you ring to ask about membership?		
4 On which day is the library open the latest?		
5 Who has free parking facilities near the library?		

6 What is wrong with the following answers?

1 Church Rd. Hove	
2 BN3 2GE	
3 290700	
4 Teusday	
5 disabled driver	

TRUE / FALSE / NOT GIVEN

You decide whether the statement agrees with or contradicts the information in the passage, or whether there is no information about the statement. The answers are in passage order but they may be grouped together in one part of the passage or spread across the passage.

How do I know if the statement is true, false or not given?

True: The statement agrees with what is in the passage, i.e. says the same thing using different words.

False: The statement contradicts what is in the passage, i.e. says the opposite.

Not Given: There is no mention of this piece of information in the passage.

Read the article below and the three statements.
Look at the explanations and answers given in the boxes.

It was not John Landy who was the first to break this record (i.e. run a mile in under four minutes) but Roger Bannister. Statement A is therefore not true but False as it contradicts the passage.

The passage refers to the 50th anniversary of the event so the answer to statement B is True.

Although you may know this to be a fact, the passage does not say that Bannister was English, so the answer to statement C is Not Given.

The four-minute mile

One of the great sporting achievements of the 20th century was when the runner Roger Bannister broke the four-minute mile record. In being the first to do so, he denied his Australian rival, John Landy, the chance of achieving immortality in the field of athletics. Media interest in the 50th anniversary of the event, including the publication of two books on the subject, highlights the significance of the achievement.

● **A** John Landy ran a mile in under four minutes before Roger Bannister.
● **B** Fifty years have passed since the four-minute mile was broken.
● **C** Roger Bannister was English.

How should I write my answers?
You only need to write T, F or NG. However, it is best to write the words in full so that your answer is clear.

ACTION PLAN

▸ Read the statements very carefully.
▸ Underline or highlight the key words or phrases in the statements and look through the passage for the first one. Often you will find the exact words, names or numbers are given to help you find the right part of the passage.
▸ Read around the words in the passage and see whether the information agrees with what is in the statement, contradicts it or whether nothing is said about it.
▸ Decide whether the answer is True, False or Not Given.

NOW TRY THE TASK

Do the following statements agree with the information given on the bank's website below?
Write

TRUE   *if the statement agrees with the information*
FALSE   *if the statement contradicts the information*
NOT GIVEN   *if there is no information on this*

Protecting you from card crime

Chip & PIN is part of an initiative across Europe to cut the rising tide of payment card fraud, which costs the UK more than £1m a day.

This new, safer card payment method proved successful during a recent trial in Northampton.

The new system uses chip technology and involves **entering your PIN into a keypad** – just as you would at a cash machine – instead of signing a till receipt whenever you pay in person in shops, restaurants and pubs etc. This is much more secure, as signatures can be easy to forge while Chip & PIN technology is extremely difficult for criminals to crack.

This means it's more important than ever to **remember your PIN**.

As your existing cards approach their expiry dates, we'll send out new Chip & PIN cards. There's no need to do anything now. We'll send your new card together with the information you need when your old cards expire.

Find out more

Read frequently asked questions about Chip & PIN and more about the programme on the Chip & PIN website.

T **7** Crime involving credit cards is increasing in Europe.
   8 The Chip & PIN system has been tested in at least one town.
   9 When you use Chip & PIN, you need to sign for your purchase.
  10 If you forget your PIN, the bank can provide a new one.
  11 The bank is advising customers to get rid of their old credit cards now.

▶▶▶▶▶▶▶▶▶▶▶▶▶▶▶▶▶

SENTENCE COMPLETION

You complete the sentences by writing up to three words and/or a number from the passage in the gaps. The gaps can come at the beginning, in the middle or at the end of the sentence. The answers are in passage order.

What is involved in sentence completion?
You need to read the sentence quickly to get the general idea, then try to predict the kind of words that are missing before you look for the answers.

Read the sentences below and decide what type of information is missing, e.g. place name, date, noun, adjective, etc. Make a note in the box.

12 The car is recommended for .... journeys.
13 Prices in the furniture sale have been cut by .... per cent.
14 Items the company can repair include .... and ....

12 ....
13 ....
14 ....

How should I write my answers?

You should only use words from the passage, and you must use no more words than you are told to use. They should be written exactly as they are in the reading passage (numbers too) and they have to be spelt correctly. Do not include unnecessary words, or repeat words that are already provided in the sentence.

ACTION PLAN

▶ Read the instructions carefully to see how many words you can write.

▶ Note the position of the gaps in the sentences.

▶ Start with the first question and decide what kind of word is needed to complete the sentence.

▶ Note any grammatical clues, e.g. articles or prepositions, which may help you find the answer.

▶ Underline or highlight the key words around each gap and use these to find the right part of the passage.

▶ Decide exactly which words or numbers you should write as the answer.

▶ Read the completed sentence to make sure that it is grammatically correct and makes sense.

NOW TRY THE TASK

Complete the sentences below which are based on the four-minute mile passage on page 36.
Choose **NO MORE THAN THREE WORDS FROM THE PASSAGE** .

15 Roger Bannister's achievement took place during the ....

16 Running was a highly competitive area of ....

17 A couple of .... were produced to celebrate the anniversary.

▶▶▶▶▶▶▶▶▶▶▶▶▶▶▶▶

NOTES / TABLE / FLOW CHART COMPLETION

You complete the gaps in the notes, table or flow chart using up to three words and/or a number from the passage. Some of the information may already be included as a guide. The answers may not be in passage order.

How are these question types different from sentence completion?

The questions are not full sentences, so you need not worry about the grammatical correctness of a sentence.

ACTION PLAN

▶ Follow the Action Plan for sentence completion above and write your answers in the same way. If you are completing a table, look at the table headings to help you decide what sort of words to look for.

▶ Remember that you may have to read above and below the first answer in the passage.

Section 1

NOW TRY THE TASK

Complete the flow chart below.
Choose **NO MORE THAN TWO WORDS AND/OR A NUMBER** *from the passage for each answer.*

Applying for a Tourist Visa Extension

Make sure your **(18)** ……. is up to date.

↓

Complete and sign **(19)** ……. (Application to stay as a visitor).

↓

Prepare all the **(20)** ……. needed for your application.

Submit the above:

↙   ↘

at your nearest **(21)** …….   by post (include a **(22)** ……. envelope).

If you are already the holder of a valid Visitor/Tourist visa, you can make an application for an extension of your visa online. Other methods are as follows.

Ensure, first of all, that you have a valid passport and that it does not need renewing before you make the application. You can include in your application any children on your passport travelling with you. You need to fill out Form 601, which can be accessed as a PDF file on the website, and add this, with a signature at the bottom, to the supporting documents listed on the next page. Do not supply original documents with your visitor application unless requested by the department, but if things like health insurance policies or custody arrangements for children are in languages other than English, they must be accompanied by a certified English translation.

Take everything, including the relevant charges, to an Immigration Office in your area – you must do this in person. Or mail your application with a stamped addressed envelope to this office.

▶▶▶▶▶▶▶▶▶▶▶▶▶▶▶▶▶▶

LABELLING A DIAGRAM

You name parts of a diagram using up to three words and/or a number from the passage. The parts to be labelled will have an arrow and the question number beside them. The answers may not be in passage order. However, the answers are usually grouped together in one part of the passage, where the diagram is described.

How should I write my answers?
You should only use words from the passage, and you must use no more words than you are told to use. They should be written exactly as they are in the reading passage (numbers too) and they have to be spelt correctly.

ACTION PLAN

▶ Read the instructions carefully to see how many words you can write.
▶ Look at the diagram to form a general idea of the content.
▶ Note any labels provided already, as these can help you find the answer.
▶ Look at the parts of the diagram to be labelled and decide what kind of information is needed to fill the gap, e.g. a place, a process, etc.
▶ Use any words provided in the diagram to find the right part of the passage.
▶ Pay particular attention to expressions of place such as *in the middle, in the corner, beyond this, next to, above/below, leads to*, etc., as the answer to the questions may depend on your understanding these concepts.

NOW TRY THE TASK

Label the diagram below .
*Choose **NO MORE THAN TWO** words from the passage for each answer.*

Sports centre

The sports centre is situated in a scenic, rural spot only ten minutes from the nearest station and with good bus links. It comprises a 25-metre swimming pool, which is heated to 21 degrees in winter, with a diving board at the north end and tiered seating on the left hand side of the pool.

On the opposite side of the complex you will find the squash courts situated in a large square building, and next to this is the gymnasium. This is where the aerobics classes take place. Between the gymnasium and the pool there is a courtyard with tables and chairs just in front of a small restaurant where you can buy sandwiches and refreshments. The whole complex is surrounded by trees.

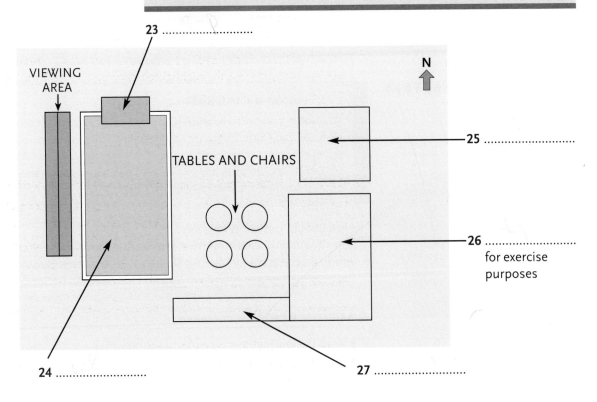

23 ....

VIEWING AREA

N

TABLES AND CHAIRS

25 ....

26 ....
for exercise purposes

24 ....

27 ....

ANSWERS PAGE 104
PRACTICE TEST PAGE 92

General Training Reading Section 2

Section 1	13–14 questions	Up to three short passages	Total 600 words maximum
Section 2	13–14 questions	Two passages	Total 750 words maximum
Section 3	13–14 questions	One long passage	Total 1000 words maximum

What are the Section 2 passages about?
Section 2 passages are all based on student, educational or work-related contexts. They come from college websites, handbooks, manuals and other informational materials.

Question Types and Practice Tasks

PARAGRAPH HEADINGS

You choose the correct heading for each paragraph from a list of headings. There are always more headings than you need, so you will not need to use them all. You will never need to use a heading more than once. There may be some example headings too, so don't use these headings again.

What is a heading?
A heading covers the main idea of the paragraph.

1 Which of these three headings states the main idea in this extract from a college website? Use the highlighted key words to help you decide.

   i How do students apply?
   ii How are students selected?
   iii How can students change courses?

There are a range of factors that are considered for entry, the main one being students' high school results. We number all students applying for a place using an internal ranking system and this is then referred to by course tutors and administrators when they choose interviewees. Some courses also assess candidates for suitability using a Baseline Admissions Test (BAT), or by requiring them to do a presentation.

2 How did the highlighted words help you?
3 Can you explain why the other headings are attractive, but wrong?

How should I write my answers?
You only need to write the correct number, i, ii, iii, etc. Don't waste time copying out the headings.

ACTION PLAN

▶ Read all the headings and underline or highlight the key words.
▶ Read the first paragraph, marking the topic sentence(s) and related phrases and vocabulary.
▶ Re-phrase the main idea of the paragraph in your mind.
▶ Read the list of headings to see if there is a match between the key words in the headings and the words you have marked in the paragraph.
▶ Choose the heading that best summarises the main idea of the first paragraph.
▶ Go on to the next paragraph and repeat the Action Plan.
▶ If you think two headings fit one paragraph, mark both of them and rule one of these out later.

NOW TRY THE TASK

*Choose the correct heading for paragraphs **A–C** from the list of headings below.*

List of Headings	
i View the whole property carefully	**4** Paragraph A
ii Being considerate may help	**5** Paragraph B
iii Check safety features	**6** Paragraph C
iv Think about the location	
v Discuss facilities with the occupants	

Finding accommodation

A Do not always assume that just because you have been provided with the written details of a property by an agent or landlord that it will meet your requirements. Ask yourself: if you move there, will you spend a fortune going to see your friends or going to college? Is there a bus route nearby? How safe is the area after midnight? If you have any doubts, phone the agent or landlord before going to look.

B Turning up at a property without an appointment does frequently work but bear in mind the inconvenience you may cause any current tenants. Don't be surprised if they won't let you in. If there is a lot of competition for the property, you may find that the landlords or agents will be more willing to deal with you if you have been polite enough to make arrangements with them beforehand.

C Once there, take some time to make sure you look at the overall package and don't be blinded by one good feature. A house with a jacuzzi may be the envy of your friends but it isn't much good if the rest of the house is uninhabitable. There are many things you should check as you are wandering around and remember that it may be possible to negotiate some improvements with the landlord before committing yourself to a contract.

7 Explain why the extra headings are attractive, but wrong.

FINDING INFORMATION IN PARAGRAPHS

You find the paragraph that contains the information in the question. You may have to find a detail, an idea, a comparison, an example, etc. Some paragraphs may contain the information required in more than one question, while other paragraphs may not be tested.

How is this question different from paragraph headings?

Paragraph headings test your understanding of the main idea in each paragraph, so the headings are the answers. In this question type, you have to read the paragraphs to see which ones contain the information you need, so the paragraph letters are the answers. You need to use a different approach for this question type.

How should I write my answers?

You only need to write the correct paragraph letter A, B, C, etc. There is only ONE answer for each question. You may use any letter more than once.

ACTION PLAN

▶ Underline or highlight the key words in the questions.
▶ Think about the ideas and language that you need to look for.
▶ Read the first paragraph and then quickly read through all the questions.
▶ Mark any parts of the paragraph that match key words in the questions.
▶ Write the paragraph letter next to that question.
▶ Go on to the next paragraph and do the same.
▶ If you think a question can be matched to more than one paragraph, make a note of this and come back to the question later to make a decision.

NOW TRY THE TASK

Which paragraph contains the following information?
NB You may use any letter more than once.

  8 a comparison between study and leisure activities   B ....
  9 two ways of keeping a schedule   ....
  10 a recommendation for building world knowledge   ....
  11 an example of poor time management   ....

WHAT MAKES A GOOD STUDENT?

A The successful student knows what to do when. Sometimes this means making a list of tasks or using an electronic diary. It doesn't matter how you achieve this, the important thing is that you don't wake up one morning with an essay to write by lunchtime; you will only do it badly.

B You need to have a genuine desire to learn. If you take up golf but you don't really care how good you are, then the chances are that you won't ever do better than average. The same is true of your course work. If you have a teacher that you don't like, or a course book that doesn't engage you, it's still necessary to apply yourself and prove to yourself that you can do well.

C You should certainly know what is going on around you and increase your understanding of this. When taking a science course, for example, it's a good idea to relate scientific principles to phenomena you observe in everyday life, and go out of your way to find applications and examples of science outside your course work.

12 Show how you got your answers by matching key words in the questions to language in the paragraphs.

Questions	Paragraphs
8 comparison /study / leisure	the same is true / golf / course work
9	
10	
11	

MATCHING

You match statements to items in a box. The statements are usually numbered 1, 2, 3, etc. and the items in the box are usually labelled A, B, C, etc. There may not be a matching statement for every item in the box, while you may need to use some items in the box more than once. The items in the box are usually in passage order, but the statements are in random order.

What sort of things can be matched?
There are many possibilities. You may have to match courses to descriptions, events to places, features to buildings, etc.

How should I write my answers?
You only need to write the correct letter (A, B, C, etc.). There is only ONE answer for each question. You may use any letter more than once.

ACTION PLAN

▶ Start with the items in the box because these are usually in passage order. Underline or highlight these in the passage. Some of the items may appear more than once in the passage, so it is important to find them all.
▶ Carefully read the statements and mark the key words.
▶ Read around the first item (A) you have marked in the passage and read the list of statements quickly to see whether any of them matches. If A occurs in other parts of the passage, read around these parts too.
▶ Write the letter A next to the correct statement(s).
▶ Repeat this procedure with the next item in the boxed list.
▶ If you think two items fit any of the statements, you will need to come back to these, as there is only one answer for each statement.

NOW TRY THE TASK

Look at the following statements (Questions 13–17) and the list of Western Institute campuses below.
Match each statement with the correct campus A–D.

Western Institute services some of the country's most isolated communities. An increasing proportion of the courses are offered flexibly and online to meet the diverse needs of the region's communities.

- **Bradyhurst Campus** A major centre for trade courses, as well as courses in business, computing and management. Specialises in bricklaying, carpentry and surveying.
- **Barlow Campus** Focuses on special programs for the local community in agriculture, business services and computing, as well as adult basic education skills, e.g. remedial reading.
- **West Hills Campus** Provides certificate and some diploma level courses in horticulture, art and design, ceramics, community services, computing, tourism and hospitality.
- **Darling Campus** A major regional centre offering access and foundation courses, accounting, business services, computing and management programs. Offers a wide range of trade courses, including motor mechanics, automotive, and other vehicle painting and panel beating programs.

A Bradyhurst	**13** suitable for students interested in cars
B Barlow	**14** offers two levels of qualification
C West Hills	**15** aimed at people wanting a career in the travel business
D Darling	**16** suitable for people interested in learning a building trade
	17 offers literacy classes

▶▶▶▶▶▶▶▶▶▶▶▶▶▶▶▶▶▶▶

CLASSIFICATION

You decide which category some statements belong to, e.g. descriptions, features, ideas, conditions, etc. The categories are usually labelled A, B, C, etc. The statements are usually numbered 1, 2, 3, etc. The answers are not in passage order.

What is classification?

In both classification and matching tasks, you have to match things together. However, in classification you may have *both/all* and *neither/none* options.

Imagine you are choosing between two jobs – Job A and Job B – and there are certain conditions that you are looking for. You could write down the conditions as statements and then match them to the jobs on offer.

1 pays more than $100 per day
2 offers more than 30 days annual leave
3 operates a flexitime system

Job A

Earn $150 plus a day, five days a week, in this fast-paced advertising company. If you're prepared to do long hours for a good salary, call now.

Job B

Fed up with working late and getting no time off? Join Pelly's and Co. and get 40 days holiday a year plus an income in excess of $120 a day.

Condition 1 is true of both jobs, condition 2 is true of Job B and condition 3 is true of neither job. This is a way of classifying the conditions.

How should I write my answers?
You only need to write the correct letter (A, B, C, etc.).

ACTION PLAN

▶ Underline or highlight the categories in the passage. These are often names. Sometimes they are used as headings (as in the example below); sometimes they are found within a longer section of the passage.
▶ Underline or highlight the key words in the statements.
▶ Read around each category in the passage and re-read the first statement. Check whether any (or none) of the language in the passage relates to the ideas in the statement. Then decide which category is correct for that statement.
▶ If you have *both* and/or *neither* categories, you need to check the information in the passage for these too.

NOW TRY THE TASK

Classify the features as being true of

A Course 1113 only   **B** Course 1345 only   **C** Both courses   **D** Neither course

18 courses offered cost less than $50 per session   D
19 personalised training is part of the program   ....
20 people can attend at weekends   ....
21 courses focus on improving photography techniques   ....

Course 1113
This course teaches you all about how to open a photographic studio and run it. Prices are in the region of $200 for a Saturday/Sunday session and evening classes are also available depending on demand. All sessions are held in groups and the aim is for students to learn from each other's experience and knowledge of the world of photography.

Answer to question 18 is **D** – neither course.

Course 1345
Find out how to take better pictures in this short weekend workshop, run by experienced staff who provide one-to-one tuition. All levels welcome. Prices start at $100 per workshop.

Check your answers by putting a ✓ or ✗ in the boxes below under each course and write the letter A, B, C or D as the answer.

Features	Course 1113	Course 1345	Answer
18 costs less than $50 per session	✗	✗	D
19 offers personalised training			
20 is run at weekends			
21 focuses on improving photography techniques			

How should I write my answers?
You only need to write the correct letter (A, B, C or D).

ACTION PLAN

▶ Underline or highlight the key words in the first question or unfinished statement.

▶ Match these key words to words in the passage so that you are looking in the right place for the answers.

▶ Underline or highlight the key words in the options and re-phrase the ideas in your mind.

▶ Read around the section of text you have marked and see if you can find words or expressions that match the options.

▶ Some word matches will occur, but check whether the passage is stating the same or something different from what is stated in the options.

NOW TRY THE TASK

Choose the correct letter A, B, C or D.

22 According to the writer, how do many people start their further education?

> *start . . . education* and *begin our education* match, so in a longer passage this is where the answer will be.

A   They have insufficient study time.
B   They cannot tell fact from opinion.
C   They need interpreters for some courses.
D   They have a subjective view of learning.

Most of us begin our education with an 'egocentric' view, expecting everything to have some relevance to our needs.
We even impose such interpretations on things we learn, and avoid learning some things because they don't seem important at the time. Education can broaden that view, encouraging us to objectively evaluate facts and information. We find out that mere unsupported, personal opinions have no value in an academic discussion.

23 It helps to re-phrase the options. Try doing this to confirm your answer. Write your version in the box.

A	*They are too busy doing other things to study.*
B	
C	
D	

PICK FROM A LIST

You pick the correct answers from a list of options. There are usually two or three answers to pick from about six options, but there may be more. The options are labelled A, B, C, etc. The answers may not be in passage order.

How is this question different from multiple choice?
In multiple choice you only pick one correct answer, and the answers to each question are in one small area of the passage. In pick from a list you pick a number of answers (usually two or three) from a list of five or six options, and you may need to read a larger area of the passage.

How should I write my answers?
You only need to write the correct letter (A, B, C, etc.). You can write these in any order. Sometimes a question is worth one mark (for finding all the answers) and sometimes the question is worth one mark for each correct answer, so be careful how you fill in your answer sheet.

ACTION PLAN

▸ Read the question carefully and note how many options you must pick and how many marks they are worth.
▸ Underline or highlight the key words in the question and options.
▸ Read the passage and find words or expressions that match the options.
▸ Check that the options you choose mean the same as in the passage.

NOW TRY THE TASK

Questions 24 and 25

*Choose **TWO** letters A–E.*

*Which **TWO** strategies for reading are recommended by the writer?*

A summarise the material verbally
B look up words you don't know
C read to the end
D make some written notes
E leave difficult sections until later

strategies and *methods* match, so in a longer passage this is where the answer will be.

If you are faced with having to read difficult material for your studies, there are several methods you can use to improve your reading skills. For a start, don't expect to find everything in an article or book difficult; there will be some parts that you can understand so you should concentrate on these at first and then come back to the trickier material and read that in more detail when you have time. That way you will get an overview of the text, and it is important to have this if you are going to understand it or write about it. So don't give up half way, and avoid using a dictionary to find out the meaning of vocabulary – use your word guessing skills instead. This will save you valuable time.

26 Which phrases in the passage match the two answers?

ANSWERS PAGE 104
PRACTICE TEST PAGE 95

General Training Reading Section 3

Section 1	13–14 questions	Up to three short passages	Total 600 words maximum
Section 2	13–14 questions	Two passages	Total 750 words maximum
Section 3	**13–14 questions**	**One long passage**	**Total 1000 words maximum**

What are the Section 3 passages about?

Section 3 consists of one complete passage on a topic of general interest. It could come from a magazine, journal, newspaper, textbook, etc.

Question Types and Practice Tasks

YES / NO / NOT GIVEN

You decide whether the statement agrees with or contradicts the writer's views or claims, or whether there is no information relating to the statement in the passage. The answers are in passage order but they may be grouped together in one part of the passage or spread across the passage.

How is this different from True / False / Not Given?

True / False / Not Given tests how well you understand factual information in the passage, whereas Yes / No / Not Given tests your understanding of the writer's views or claims. However, the approach to the two question types is the same.

What are the writer's views or claims?

Many passages include the writer's opinion (views or claims) on a topic as well as providing factual information. Views or claims are sometimes marked by sentence openers such as *It seems that*. This is more common in spoken English, however. In written English, individual words such as *surprising*, *unusual*, *appear*, etc. are more likely to convey opinions. A statement that cannot be supported by facts is generally the writer's view.

1 Which of the following statements contain the writer's view?
   a Meakins was an exceptionally good cabinetmaker.
   b This year, the music industry has experienced a decline in the sale of CDs.
   c Much of the art we see in exhibitions around the world is unimpressive.
   d Scientists believe they may have discovered a cure for the common cold.
   e In future, we should aim to develop our alternative energy supplies.

What if I think I know the answer from my general knowledge?

You must only answer using the information you read in the passage. If you think you know the answer but it does not appear in the passage, the answer must be Not Given.

2 Read this extract about security systems. Underline or highlight two views or claims made by the writer. Is the majority of the passage the writer's opinion, or is it mostly factual information?

🔒 THE TWO SIDES TO SECURITY 🔓

In the security industry today, there are two clear divisions and one of these is decidedly more glamorous than the other. The glamorous part deals with digital security, which includes everything from fighting computer viruses and tackling malicious computer hackers to controlling which employees have access to which systems. All of this has overshadowed the less glamorous side of the industry, which deals with physical security – in essence, door locks, alarms and that sort of thing. The people involved in digital security come across as bright and interesting, whereas the door-lock people do not. This second group soon have to admit that there have been no real advances in locks since the invention of the pin-tumbler lock, which was actually devised in ancient Egypt but was then lost until Mr Linus Yale, an American inventor, rediscovered it. And even that was a century and a half ago.

How do I match the views to the statements?

The statements make one clear point. You decide whether they agree with or contradict the views expressed in the passage, or whether the writer has given no information about that point.

Read the passage above and the three statements below. Decide which one
- agrees with the writer (Y)
- contradicts the writer (N)
- is based on information not found in the passage (NG).

3 Designing ways to protect computers from hackers represents the boring side of the security industry.

4 Conventional door-locking mechanisms have changed very little in the last century.

5 Linus Yale worked on the pin-tumbler lock alone.

How should I write my answers?

You only need to write the letters Y, N or NG. However, it is best to write the words in full so that your answer is clear.

ACTION PLAN

▶ Read the first statement carefully and re-phrase it in your own words.
▶ Underline or highlight the key words or phrases in the first statement and quickly read the passage for these. Often you will find the same words, names or numbers in the passage. This is done to help you find the idea or information and get started in the right part of the passage.
▶ Read around the words in the passage and see whether the view that is expressed agrees with what is in the statement, contradicts it, or whether nothing is said about it.

NOW TRY THE TASK

Do the following statements reflect the claims of the writer in the passage below?
Write

YES	*if the statement reflects the claims of the writer*
NO	*if the statement contradicts the claims of the writer*
NOT GIVEN	*if it is impossible to say what the writer thinks about this*

6 Most new motor vehicles are fitted with remote locks.
7 Hotel guests prefer conventional room keys to plastic ones.
8 Hotels appreciate the benefits of computerised room keys.
9 All dwellings will soon be fitted with electronic keys.

DIGITAL SECURITY

Digital security systems are no longer the stuff of science-fiction movies. Fortunately, we can now enjoy the fact that electronic doors in office blocks and apartment buildings are standard fittings, as are remote locking systems for most new cars.

International hotel chains have for many years embraced the idea of computerised security systems, and guests are issued, not with a key, but with a plastic card programmed to function for the limited period of their stay, with the result that troublesome or non-paying hotel guests can be locked out of their rooms at the touch of a keyboard, and lost keys no longer represent a security risk. Great for the hotel management, which no longer has to worry about people going home with the keys!

But despite the availability of these high-tech security systems, most private homes today still use conventional locks, possibly because we enjoy the mechanical satisfaction of turning the key. The front door key has yet to be replaced by the plastic swipe card, and I doubt it will in the foreseeable future.

10 Underline or highlight the words in the passage which gave you the answers.
11 Re-write questions 6–9 so that they have the opposite meaning.

SENTENCE COMPLETION WITH A BOX

You choose the correct ending from a box of options to make a complete sentence which contains an idea from the passage. There will be some extra endings that you do not need to use. You may be able to use some of the endings more than once. The answers are in passage order.

How is this different from sentence completion without a box?

In sentence completion without a box, you only have to find a detail in the passage and write the correct word or words to complete a sentence. Here, you have to join two parts of a sentence together to make one sentence that paraphrases an idea in the passage. You need to use a different approach for this question type so that the completed sentence makes logical sense and is grammatically correct.

A for his own orchestras.
B to enhance the cultural image of the city.
C as a way of saving money.

12 Complete this sentence with the ending A, B or C that is most likely to be correct.

The new Concert Hall was built

13 Explain why the other endings are wrong.

How should I write my answers?

You only need to write the correct letters A, B, C, etc. Usually the endings are only used once. If you need to use an ending more than once, the instructions will tell you.

ACTION PLAN

▶ Read the first unfinished statement carefully and underline or highlight the key words.
▶ Use the key words in the unfinished statement to find the idea in the passage.
▶ Read around the information in the passage to make sure you understand it.
▶ Quickly read the list of endings and underline or highlight the key words.
▶ Choose the ending which best fits the idea in the passage.
▶ Make sure the ending is logical and fits grammatically.

NOW TRY THE TASK

*Complete each sentence with the correct ending **A–F** below.*
NB *You may use any ending more than once.*

Walt Disney Concert Hall

THE LATEST ARCHITECTURAL MASTERPIECE BY FRANK GEHRY ADDS MUCH-NEEDED CIVIC PRIDE TO LOS ANGELES

It was only a matter of time before downtown Los Angeles got a facelift. One look at the gleaming new building on the corner of First Street and Grand Avenue and it's clear why the area is experiencing such a revival. The building in question is the award-winning architect Frank Gehry's latest masterpiece, the Walt Disney Concert Hall. Gehry, who used to live in Los Angeles, wanted the Hall to look like no other concert hall built in the last 20 years.

This unusual building is soon to become home to the Los Angeles Philharmonic Orchestra. The steel exterior is in sharp contrast to the warm, wooded interior of the main concert hall. The incredible 6,125 pipe organ is a dramatic focal point and resembles a collection of sticks in a bundle. To ensure that the acoustics were absolutely right, fifty models were built and precise tests carried out before the design was finalised.

A sculpted fountain created by Gehry is the centrepiece of the garden. It is made from 200 tiny pieces of china and is in memory of Lillian Disney's love of Delft pottery and gardening. The piece adds a soft natural touch to the otherwise stark exterior of the building.

A a cleverly designed organ.
B a new civic look.
C a member of the LA Philharmonic.
D a sculpture designed by the architect.
E a piece of Delft pottery.
F a former resident of the city.

14 Los Angeles has recently received
15 Frank Gehry is
16 The most eye-catching part of the concert hall is
17 The focal point of the garden is

SUMMARY COMPLETION

You complete the summary by writing no more than three words and/or a number from the passage in each gap. The summary may cover the ideas in the whole passage or may be based on a section of the passage only. You may be told which part it relates to. The answers may not be in passage order.

What is summary completion?

It is similar to sentence completion, but here, you also need to pay attention to how the ideas are linked together.

18 Read the summary below and decide what type of information is missing. Look at the highlighted words to help you do this. What do the words *But this tiny* tell you about the type of answer needed in Question 19? What does the word *they* tell you about the type of answer needed in Question 20? Make a note of the type of word you predict for each answer.

19	Few people have ever heard of Yonaguni, in Japan's Okinawa island chain. But this tiny **(19)** ...... has recently attracted international attention after the discovery of **(20)** .... Locals believe they are the remnants of a vast civilisation lost many years ago. The site is now a popular destination for **(21)** ...... who like an underwater challenge.
20	
21	

How should I write my answers?

You should only use words from the passage, and you must use no more words than you are told to use. They should be written exactly as they are in the reading passage (numbers too) and they have to be spelt correctly. Do not include unnecessary words, or repeat words that are already provided.

ACTION PLAN

▶ Read the instructions carefully to see how many words you can write, and whether you are told which paragraph(s) the summary comes from.

▶ Read the summary heading (if there is one) to help you find the right place in the passage.

▶ Read through the summary to get an idea of what it is about and how much of the passage it covers.

▶ Decide what kind of word is needed to complete the first gap, e.g. a noun, a name, an adjective.

▶ Note any grammatical clues, e.g. articles or prepositions, which may help you find the answer.

▶ Underline or highlight the key words around the gap.

▶ Read the passage quickly and decide where the answer to the first question comes from.

▶ Decide exactly which words or numbers you should write as your answer.

▶ Read above and below this part to find the rest of the answers.

NOW TRY THE TASK

Complete the summary below.
*Choose **NO MORE THAN TWO WORDS AND/OR A NUMBER** from the reading passage for each answer.*

Sprawling systems on the edge of IT chaos

The UK government is at the forefront of a £10 million programme aimed at finding ways to stop catastrophic failures occurring in large IT networks. Some systems are now so large they are untestable, making it impossible to predict how they will behave under all circumstances. The hidden errors could lead to crashes in critical networks like healthcare or banking systems.

The scheme has been given added urgency by the failures of power grids in the US and Italy last year. 'The system failures in terms of electricity blackouts show that patterns of unexpected and negative behaviour can arise, and when they do they are often disastrous,' says the government's chief scientist, David King. If a century-old technology like a power grid can fail, the same might easily happen to modern IT networks.

Taking precautions

The government has set up a scheme at a cost of **(22)** ...... to investigate ways of preventing large IT **(23)** .... Because they are very **(24)** ......, the systems cannot always be tested and the fear is that hidden problems could interrupt essential services such as health and **(25)** .... According to the government's chief scientist, the effects of these electricity blackouts could be **(26)** ....

27 Find words or phrases in the reading passage about IT networks that have been replaced by the following words in the summary.

a scheme	
b investigate ways of preventing	
c cannot always be tested	
d essential services	
e According to	

SUMMARY COMPLETION WITH A BOX

You complete the gaps in the summary by choosing the correct option from a box of options. These are usually single words but they may be short phrases. There will be some extra words in the box that you do not need to use. The summary may cover the ideas in the whole passage or may be based on a section of the passage only. You may be told which part it relates to.

How is this different from summary completion without a box?

You should follow the **Action Plan** on page 53, but you also need to match the ideas in the passage to the correct words in the box. This means that you will need to recognise synonyms or words that paraphrase ideas in the passage.

28 Look at the words *in italics* in B and underline or highlight the words in A that they have replaced.

A

Coral bleaching occurs when the important algae that live in corals become stressed and are expelled. This turns corals white, leaving them in an unhealthy state.

B

If *essential organisms* are *lost* from a coral reef, a process called coral bleaching can *take place*, which *renders* corals white and unhealthy.

29 What does *this* refer to in A?
30 What does *which* refer to in B?

How should I write my answers?

You only need to write the letters A, B, C, etc. Do not waste time copying out the words as well.

NOW TRY THE TASK

Read the passage on page 54.
Complete the summary using the list of words A–J.

A test	**F** repair
B build	**G** priority
C measure	**H** importance
D age	**I** funding
E size	**J** condition

The government has established a £10 million programme designed to prevent potentially catastrophic IT failures. This is because the **(31)** ...... of some systems makes it very difficult to **(32)** ...... them accurately. The idea has been given **(33)** ...... following the electrical failures in America and Europe last year, which were due to the considerable **(34)** ...... of the grids.

35 Which words in the passage helped you choose the correct words from the box?

ANSWERS PAGE 105
PRACTICE TEST PAGE 97

The General Training Writing Test

A 60-minute test of your ability to write in English

How many parts does the writing test have?
There are two tasks but Task 2 is worth more marks than Task 1, so it is important to try to keep to the recommended timing for each one.

Task 1 (about 20 minutes)
You write a 150-word letter according to the bullet-pointed instructions you are given.

Task 2 (about 40 minutes)
You write a discursive essay of 250 words in response to a question or argument on a general topic.

What is the writing test like?
You will receive a question paper with two writing tasks on it and an answer sheet. The tasks are not related in any way and require quite different answers. You must write your answers to both tasks within the hour.

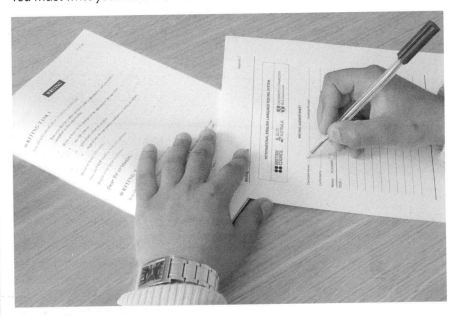

Is there any choice of tasks?
No. You have to do the two tasks you are given.

Why are there two tasks in the writing test?
It is important that the examiner can see how good you are at different types of writing. You have to show how well you can write a letter. You also have to show that you can write a clear, well-structured essay.

How is the writing test marked?
The writing test is marked using a 9-band scale, like all other parts of the test. The examiner will be looking at four features of your written language: **content**, **organisation**, **vocabulary** and **grammar**.

📄 ON THE DAY

- The writing test is the third part of the IELTS test. It takes place after the reading test on the same day.

- You receive a question paper and an answer sheet that has enough space to write your answer to both tasks.

- You can write in pencil or pen.

- You cannot use rough paper but you can write on the question paper.

- If you make any notes on the answer sheet, cross them out before you hand it in.

- You can ask the administrator for an extra answer sheet if you need it.

- Make sure you write the answer to each task in the correct section of the booklet.

- You will get time checks after 20 minutes and just before the end of the whole test.

- You must stop writing after one hour or you may be disqualified.

- You cannot leave the room until the test is over.

Content	Is the **content** of your answer accurate, relevant and appropriate?		**Vocabulary**	Is your choice of **vocabulary** appropriate and have you used words accurately?
Task 1	Is the purpose of your letter clear? Have you covered all three bullet points? Have you developed these points enough? Have you used the right tone? Have you written in letter format?			Have you used a range of appropriate words and expressions? Have you used some idiomatic or less common expressions? Have you avoided repeating the same words? Have you used words in their correct forms? Is your spelling accurate?
Task 2	Have you made your position clear? Are the main ideas clear? Are the ideas well supported? Is there a relevant conclusion?			
Organisation	Is the **organisation** of your answer clear and logical? Is the development of the whole answer logical? Have you used paragraphs appropriately? Are the sentences well linked to each other? Are the links between ideas clear?		**Grammar**	Is your choice of sentences and structures varied and is your **grammar** accurate? Have you used complex and simple sentences? Have you used a range of accurate structures? Can the examiner understand what you mean? Is your punctuation accurate?

What if I don't understand the tasks?

You cannot ask the administrator any questions about the tasks. If you do not understand, you should at least write something based on the task and topic. By doing this, you will lose fewer marks, because answers that are on a different topic, or that are memorised, lose a lot of marks.

What general approach should I take to the writing test?

As there are two tasks in the writing test, timing is very important. You must make sure you leave enough time to complete Task 2 because it is worth more marks than Task 1.

You must answer the questions you are asked. For Task 1, you must remember who you are writing the letter to and write in an appropriate style, making sure you cover all three bullet points. For Task 2, read the question carefully and then write your answer on the topic, making sure you support all your points. Follow the instructions given. Leave time at the end of the test to read through your answers and check for mistakes.

Can I write in note form?

No. You should write a letter for Task 1 and an essay for Task 2. For both tasks, your sentences should be complete and organised into clear paragraphs. Answers that are written as notes lose marks and you cannot get a high mark for organisation if you do not use paragraphs.

Can I write in capital letters?

You should avoid writing in capital letters because the examiner needs to know whether you can punctuate your work and use capital letters correctly.

What if I write under or over the word limits?

You should try to keep to the word limits. If you write too few words, you will lose marks. There are no extra marks for writing more, so if you have time to spare, use this to check through what you have written, rather than writing extra.

How can I improve my score in the writing test?

You can help to improve your score by making sure that you know what types of writing you will be expected to do and what the examiner will be looking for. The following pages, divided into Task 1 and Task 2, cover these points thoroughly and provide you with an **Action Plan** for each task.

General Training Writing Task 1

Task 1	150 words	20 minutes	Letter
Task 2	250 words	40 minutes	Discursive essay

What do I have to do in Task 1?
The instructions give you a situation and tell you who to write your letter to. There are three related bullet points and you must fully cover each one in a total of 150 words.

What type of letter will I have to write?
This depends on the task. It could be an informal letter to a friend or a more formal one to someone you don't know. For example, you may need to write to a friend about some holiday plans (informal) or request assistance or information from a government office (formal). You do not need to include your address at the top of the letter.

CONTENT

You must cover and develop all three bullet points in the task and make the purpose of your letter clear. Your answer must be appropriate in tone (formal/informal style) and format (a letter of continuous writing, not notes) for the situation. It should also be relevant to the task.

How can I make sure I answer all parts of the task?
You should analyse the task carefully to understand the situation, and see how the three bullet points relate to it.

Look at the notes on task A.

A

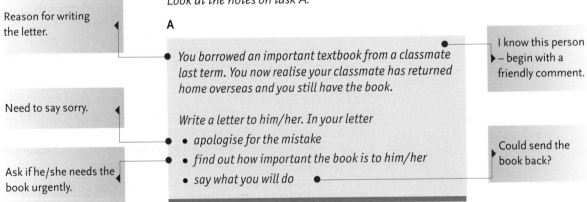

Reason for writing the letter.

Need to say sorry.

Ask if he/she needs the book urgently.

You borrowed an important textbook from a classmate last term. You now realise your classmate has returned home overseas and you still have the book.

Write a letter to him/her. In your letter
- *apologise for the mistake*
- *find out how important the book is to him/her*
- *say what you will do*

I know this person – begin with a friendly comment.

Could send the book back?

Do I need to cover the points in the order they appear in the task?
No, but you should cover them all in your answer and give enough detail, otherwise you will lose marks. You may need to write more on some points than others.

What if I can't think of anything to write?
Remember that the three bullet points are there to help you. Use your imagination and note down some ideas on each point before you begin to write. Here are some notes a student has made for task A.

Task	Do I know the reader?	Begin and end?	Point 1	Point 2	Point 3	Concluding paragraph
A	Yes	Dear Yuki Best wishes	Apologise – borrowed book for exams	Does she need the book for studies now?	Send by mail or send money instead?	Will wait to hear before deciding what to do
B						
C						

1 Read tasks B and C and make notes like the ones for task A above in the table.

B

You have received a letter from your bank, asking you to acknowledge receipt of a new bank card. However, the card was missing from the envelope.

Write a letter to the bank's head office. In your letter
- explain why you are writing
- express concern about the missing card
- ask them what they intend to do

C

You have recently been to stay with an old friend for a few days. You hadn't seen each other for a long time.

Write a letter to the friend. In your letter
- say how you felt about the visit
- refer to something enjoyable that you did while staying with him/her
- invite your friend to visit you

How should I begin and end the letter?

If you know the name of the person, you can begin and end your letter like this:

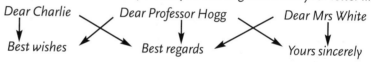

Don't use the given name and family names together, e.g. Dear Mr ~~John~~ Liu.
If you don't know the name of the person you are writing to, then write:
    Dear Sir (or Madam) and Yours faithfully.

How can I make my purpose clear?

In a formal letter, begin by stating the purpose of your letter clearly so that the reader understands immediately why you are writing. In an informal letter to a friend, you can begin by referring briefly to their life or to something you have in common, before moving on to the main purpose of your letter.

2 Complete the first part of the letter for task A on page 58.

Dear Yuki,
    I hope you had a safe journey back to Japan, and that your family are all well.
    I am writing to say that I'm **(a)** .... for not giving you back the book 'English Grammar in Use' which I borrowed from you last term. You **(b)** .... it to me just before the exams to help me prepare for them, and yesterday I **(c)** .... it under my bed.

3 Underline or highlight the part that states the purpose of the letter.

How should I continue my letter?
Go back to task A on page 58 and re-read the second and third bullet points.

Highlight the key words.
• find out how important the book is to him/her
• say what you will do

Refer to the notes you made in the table on page 59. Your letter should also have a concluding paragraph.

4 Complete the rest of the letter below.

> Please **(a)** .... me know straight away if you **(b)** .... this book for your studies right now or whether you can **(c)** .... without it.
>
> If you really need it, I can **(d)** .... it to you by airmail immediately. If not, do you mind if I **(e)** .... it by ordinary mail as it is quite heavy? Or, if you prefer, I can send some **(f)** .... instead. Please let me know what you **(g)** .... me to do.
>
> I hope you enjoy the holiday.

What are the differences between formal and informal tone?
You must be clear about whether the letter is formal or informal and choose the right language. Formal letters need to be polite but to the point. Informal letters, on the other hand, can begin with a friendly opening that shows the relationship between the reader and writer.

5 Do you need a formal (F) or an informal (I) tone for the following letters?

  a Inviting your classmates to a surprise party.
  b Thanking a friend for a birthday present.
  c Writing a letter about an insurance claim.
  d Asking for an extension for an essay.
  e Telling a friend how to get to your house.
  f Asking someone to return something you lent them a year ago.

6 Look at the following sentence starters. Decide which ones would be useful in a formal letter (F) and which would be useful in an informal letter (I). Some of them may be useful in both types of letter (B).

  a I am writing to...
  b Can you... ?
  c What about... ?
  d Could you please... ?
  e Would it be possible... ?
  f Please accept my...
  g Thanks a lot for...
  h I hope you're...
  i Sorry to hear about...
  j I'm really glad...
  k I would (I'd) be grateful if you could...
  l Looking forward to...

7 Look at the tasks for letters B and C on page 59. Write a paragraph stating the purpose of each letter and covering the first point of each one.

ORGANISATION

The three bullet points are there to help you develop your letter. You don't have to write a paragraph for each point, but you should write in paragraphs and your ideas should be linked together well.

How many paragraphs do I write?

Write three to five paragraphs: your introductory paragraph, two or three paragraphs for the main part of your answer and a concluding sentence. Aim to have one main idea in each paragraph.

How can I link my ideas within paragraphs?

You can link your ideas within paragraphs by using words or phrases such as *unfortunately* and *however*. It is also sometimes useful to connect the new paragraph to the previous one using a phrase such as *As I mentioned before*.

1 Read the letter below for task B on page 59 and re-write it using the words in the box to help link the ideas. Words or punctuation which need to be changed have been highlighted.

---

it
Unfortunately,
but obviously
even though
but
which
because
which
it
Could you tell me

Dear Sir,

I am writing to inform you that I received a letter from my bank today. **(a)** .... It was supposed to contain my new bank card. **(b)** .... there was no bank card enclosed in the envelope when I opened it.

I telephoned the bank to explain the problem **(c)** .... I could not get through to the right department **(d)** .... I waited on the line for over half an hour. **(e)** .... It was extremely annoying.

In the letter, you asked me to acknowledge receipt of the card **(f)** .... I cannot do this as I have not received **(g)** the card. I am now very worried **(h)** .... there is a possibility that my card has gone to another customer or got lost. **(i)** .... what will happen if somebody has already used the card and spent my money? Will the bank repay me?

Is it possible for the bank to cancel this card so nobody else can use **(j)** the card? Could you also send me a new card by secure means?

I hope to hear from you soon.

---

2 Plan and complete a letter for task C on page 59. Here are some notes to help you.

Letter C
• writing to thank
• ....
• particularly good going to
• come and visit ....

VOCABULARY

You need to show that you have a range of vocabulary suitable for the task, and that you can use these words appropriately and accurately in your letter.

How can I make sure my vocabulary is appropriate?

Your choice of vocabulary will depend on the purpose of the letter and the relationship of the writer to the reader. Choosing the right words or expressions is an important part of getting the tone right.

1 Are the following sentences formal (F) or informal (I)? Underline or highlight the words which tell you.

  a I'm writing to enquire about the Manager's position advertised in…
  b Lovely to see you at the weekend. Thanks for a great party.
  c Thank you for sending me the copy of 'IT Journal' which I ordered last week. Unfortunately, it was damaged in the post so I'd be grateful if…
  d I'd like to apologise for my late arrival on Monday which was due to…
  e Great to catch up with you on Friday. Sorry I was a bit late.

How can I show a range of vocabulary?

Think of words that are similar in meaning to words you are given. This is called brainstorming. You can do this by writing down all the words that come into your head when you read the task. You may not use all these words.

Look at task D and the box of brainstorm words which might be useful to answer it.

D

> *You are studying overseas. You need to return to your country before the end of the semester for a family event.*
>
> *Write a letter to your supervisor. In your letter*
> - *request the time off*
> - *explain why you need to leave early*
> - *reassure him/her that your studies will not suffer*

Brainstorm words
permission to miss
have to go home
important occasion
wedding / get married
close family
sorry for the inconvenience
apologise for asking
keep up with studies
examinations
complete assignments
do the work
hope you can agree
look forward to hearing

2 Look at task E and do a vocabulary brainstorm for the letter.

E

> *You have seen an advertisement for part-time work in a hotel for three months over the summer.*
>
> *Write a letter to the Manager. In your letter*
> - *say what experience you have*
> - *ask what the work involves*
> - *enquire about conditions*

What else can I do to improve my vocabulary score?

You should try to build up your phrases by choosing words that go together well and fit the task.

3 Complete the sentences by choosing a verb and an adjective from the boxes to fill the gaps. Put the verbs in the right tense.

Verb	Adjective
make	legal
submit	unexpected
accept	genuine
receive	unforgettable
have	appalling
take	serious
show	sincere
give	online

  a Please .... my .... apologies.
  b Yesterday I .... some .... news about my family.
  c When we .... the accident, the weather was ....
  d The neighbours .... a very .... complaint about the noise.
  e I was .... some .... advice about buying a new flat.
  f The audience .... their .... enthusiasm for the play by cheering loudly.
  g The night flight we .... to the tropical island was a truly .... experience.
  h I have .... an .... application for the job.

Can I use words from the task on the question paper?

You can use individual words from the question paper, but if you copy long phrases or whole sentences, these words will be deducted from the total word count of your answer.

How important is accuracy?

You will lose marks if you write words in the wrong form, e.g. *I am writing to application*, if you choose the wrong word or if you do not spell words correctly.

4 Find the errors in letter F below.

F

Dear Dr simpson,

I am writing to apologies for not coming to the English language test last wenesday morning. I was unable to attend because my alarm clock did not go off. As a result, I slept until ten o'clock and avoided the eight o'clock train.

I wonder if it would be possible for you to give me another oportunity to pass the test? I assure you that I will work very hard and will not let you down a second time. I studied most weekend for this test to get a correct mark, so I have to say that I am really very disappointed by what happened.

It is very importance for me to do well in this course as my future depends on it. I could come to your office whatever you have the time. I would quite appreciate your help in this.

I wish to hear from you soon.

5 What do you think were the instructions for the task for letter F? Write the three bullet points. Underline or highlight the key words in the letter.

GRAMMAR

You need to show that you can use a range of sentences and structures and that you can use grammar accurately. You also need to punctuate your writing well.

How can I show a range of sentence types?

You need to write sentences that contain more than one clause. It is better to do this and make mistakes than to write in simple sentences all the time.

1 Use the words in brackets to make one complex sentence from each set of notes below.

  a emptying suitcase / found book / bottom of it (*when*)
  b come and visit us / free time / next year? (*why not*)
  c letter / you sent / arrived late / no bank card (*which*)
  d looking / hotel job / involves / administration work (*that*)
  e could / tell me / you have / part-time jobs? (*whether*)
  f need / request time off / stay with brother / wife having baby (*whose*)

How can I show a range of structures?

You should show that you can handle different tenses and are able to use conditionals, modals and auxiliary verbs.

2 Complete letter G below using verbs from the box. You can use any of these verbs more than once.

G

have
would
will
is getting
look forward
am
am writing
can

Dear Professor Hogg,

I (a) ...... to ask permission to miss the last two weeks of term because I (b) ...... to go home to my country for an important family occasion.

I (c) ...... not normally ask for time off during the semester, especially as we (d) ...... examinations early next year, but it is really important for me to be with my family.

My brother (e) ...... married at the end of October and I (f) ...... really like to be there. We're a very close family, and if I don't attend the wedding, they (g) ...... never forgive me!

I (h) ...... confident that I can keep up with the work while I am away, and I promise to complete any assignments that are due before I leave.

I hope that you (i) ...... agree to my request and I (j) ...... to hearing from you very soon. Please feel free to email me on jgood@hotmail.com

Best regards,

How important is grammatical accuracy?

You will lose marks if you make grammatical errors in your writing, particularly when the errors are frequent and affect meaning.

3 Look at letter H below, which is a sample answer to task E on page 62. Find ten grammatical errors and make the corrections.

H

Dear Sir,

I am writing to enquire about the part-time position for waiter advertised in 'The Evening Echo' on 24th June.

I look for work in the months of July and August because my university vacation is then. I have quite experience in the hotel business, as I working in a guesthouse last year. The job involved dealing with the guests, and I very much enjoyed. I can supply references from my previous employer if you require them.

Could you please let me know what this position involves? At the guesthouse, I worked as a porter, and I also did some work as a waiter in the restaurant, so I would be interesting in either of these jobs.

Could you give me an idea of the working hours? I am available at the weekends as well as during the week, and I can work any hours. However, I preferred daytime work to shifts, if possible. Could you also tell me about accommodation for employees and how much do you pay.

I would be very appreciate to hear from you.

Yours faithfully,

ACTION PLAN

▶ Read the task carefully and decide whether to write a formal or informal letter.

▶ Decide how the letter will begin.

▶ Note down your main ideas for each point and brainstorm the words you might use.

▶ Write an opening sentence or paragraph stating the purpose of your letter.

▶ Link your ideas together so that your answer is logical and clearly developed.

▶ Try to use a range of relevant vocabulary and sentence types.

▶ Finish your answer with an appropriate concluding sentence and letter ending.

▶ Leave time to check your answer for errors. Look at spelling, grammar and punctuation.

▶ Count the number of words you have used.

ANSWERS PAGE 106
PRACTICE TEST PAGE 99

General Training Writing Task 2

Task 1	150 words	20 minutes	Letter
Task 2	**250 words**	**40 minutes**	**Discursive essay**

What do I have to do in Task 2?

Task 2 is a topic on which you have to write a discursive essay. The topic may be in the form of a statement or a question. Sometimes different or opposing views are expressed; sometimes there is one view to discuss.

CONTENT

You must answer all parts of the task. You need to make your own position clear and provide main ideas and supporting arguments to illustrate this. You should write a clear introduction and conclusion.

How can I make sure I answer all parts of the task?

You should analyse the task carefully so that you know exactly what you have to write about.

Look at the notes on task A and the summary of these in the table below.

A

These are opposing views.

These days, noise and air pollution are serious environmental problems. Some people think that air travel is to blame. Others believe that we should reduce the number of vehicles on the roads.

I must discuss both views – so it would help to think about who would have these different views and why.

Discuss both these views and give your opinion.

I must say what I think.

Task	Are opposing views expressed?	What are the key words?	How many parts must I write about?
A	Yes	Noise/air pollution/ air travel / vehicles / roads	Two – air travel and road travel
B			
C			

1 Read these tasks and then complete the table on page 66.

B

> *For some people, the ideal holiday is to get away from their normal routine by staying in a hotel or camping in the countryside. Others prefer to stay at home and do things they do not normally have time for.*
>
> *What do you think are the benefits of going away on holiday?*

C

> *A lot of films are now being made strictly for the DVD market and soon we will be able to download films directly from the internet.*
>
> *How do you think this development is affecting cinema audiences? Is this a positive or a negative development?*

What is my 'position'?

Your position is your view on the topic. Make sure that you say what your position is, and that it stays the same, i.e. don't contradict yourself.

Look at task B above. Which of the following is your position?

  i There are many benefits.
 ii There are some benefits (but some drawbacks too).
iii There are no real benefits.

2 How is task C different from B?
3 What is your position likely to be on task C?

How do I make my position clear?

You should state your position clearly, perhaps as part of your introduction, support it throughout your answer and re-state it (in a different way) in the conclusion.

4 Underline or highlight the writer's position in this introduction to task B. Is it position i, ii or iii?

> Many people start their year by thinking about where they would like to go on holiday. This sort of decision is important for them because they feel they need to have a break from their regular activities. There are many advantages to this and I feel that you return to work in a better frame of mind if you have been away.

5 Change the last sentence so that the paragraph expresses position ii.
6 You need to re-state your position in the conclusion, by pulling together your main ideas and showing how they support your argument. Underline or highlight the writer's position in this conclusion.

> Although you may return from holiday to find that you have a lot of things to do, you will feel much better about doing them. The enormous benefits of spending time away from work and other domestic pressures can even mean that you enjoy taking part in your regular activities again.

7 Write your own introduction to task C.

What is a main idea?

A main idea is a key point or argument that relates directly to the question and to your position. You only need a few main ideas but remember that you may need main ideas on both sides of an argument.

8 Complete these notes, which give some main ideas for task C on page 67.

POSITIVES	NEGATIVES
Can choose from .... films	Fewer big .... will be produced
Can watch films	Harder to control what .... watch
Can .... films from the internet	Encourages more ....

What if I don't have any ideas?

If you cannot think of your own ideas, think about what you have read on the topic in books or magazines, or seen on television.

How do I make my main ideas clear?

Your main ideas should come between the introduction and conclusion and form the body of your answer. Each main idea should be in a separate paragraph.

What are supporting arguments?

Supporting arguments add extra information to your main ideas. You should link the main idea to the topic and then support it.

9 Underline or highlight the sentence which contains the supporting argument in this paragraph from task C on page 67.

> One of the advantages of the development of the DVD market is that people will eventually have a much wider range of films to choose from. Although we can watch DVDs at any time, we generally have to watch what is available in the shops. Soon, however, we may be able to download our favourite films, even if they are not well known.

10 Look at task D below. Write an introductory paragraph, and another that includes a main idea and supporting arguments.

D

In some countries, government safety laws include things such as wearing a hard hat on a building site or wearing safety clothes in certain factories.

To what extent are laws of this kind a good idea? What sort of safety law would you introduce?

ORGANISATION

Your answer needs to develop logically from your introduction through several paragraphs to your conclusion. Within the paragraphs, your ideas should be linked together well.

How do I decide how many paragraphs to write?

Write between five and seven paragraphs: your introductory paragraph, three to five paragraphs for the main body of your answer, and your concluding paragraph. Aim to have one main idea in each paragraph.

1 This long paragraph would be better if it was broken into two paragraphs. Where could you start the second paragraph? To help you decide, underline or highlight the two sentences which contain the main ideas.

We all like DVDs but there are quite a few concerns related to this market that we ought to consider. It is already said that children and some teenagers watch too much television and the expansion of the DVD market is only going to make this problem worse. Parents will find it difficult to prevent their children from watching all their favourite films, especially if their friends are doing this. How can parents control the content of the films that their children watch? At the moment, there are not too many films around and you often know what new films are about. DVDs, however, may be made by smaller film companies and may contain unsuitable material, but this may not be clearly indicated. Obviously we will need new laws to control this area.

How can I develop my answer logically?

You need to start each new paragraph with a word or phrase that shows that you are making a new or related point, e.g. *I tend to disagree with this view*. You should do this to make your ideas clear.

2 Which of the following expressions could you use to begin your second paragraph above, so that it links well to the first paragraph? (You will need to re-structure the start of the sentence a little.)

   i Another concern is

   ii I also feel that

   iii Nevertheless

   iv However

3 Complete the paragraph openers below for the task on safety laws (task D on page 68).

There are a number of reasons why safety laws are a good idea.

Paragraph 1

.... is that they save lives.

Paragraph 2

They .... protect workers who have to do dangerous jobs.

Paragraph 3

Some people, ... , argue that safety laws are unreasonable and take away our personal freedom.

How can I link my ideas within paragraphs?

You can link your ideas by using linking words and phrases, e.g. *however, yet, unfortunately, indeed, then* or *generally speaking*. Note that these words do not always have to be at the start of a sentence.

4 Here are some supporting points for the first paragraph about safety laws. Add these to the first main idea using the words given to link up the ideas.

> children in particular – cannot make decisions / because too young / so laws good

5 Another way of linking ideas is to use reference words, e.g. *these, this, one, him, such,* etc. Read the introductory paragraph below in which the reference words have been highlighted. Complete the table showing what they refer to.

In some countries, if you have a swimming pool nearby, there must be a high fence or barrier around it, even if it is in your private garden. This is to stop young children from falling in if they are playing near the pool. Regulations such as these are necessary to prevent tragedies from occurring, although they are sometimes seen as unnecessary.

it	the pool	they	
it		these	
This		they	

6 Complete the gaps in the two paragraphs below with a correct reference word from the box. Some of the words will be used more than once.

who
their
these
they
this
the
one

In my view, safety laws are very important for road travel. In many countries, governments make sure that people wear seat belts in cars by imposing heavy fines if they are found not wearing (a) .... Some people argue that (b) .... seat belt law is unnecessary but many lives have been saved and young children, (c) .... are most at risk, cannot always rely on (d) .... parents to make (e) .... decisions for them.

Another safety law that is common in many countries relates to the wearing of crash helmets on motorbikes. (f) .... vehicles can be very dangerous and motorbike riders and (g) .... passengers often have very little protection if (h) .... have an accident. Although it may be more comfortable to ride a bike without a helmet, it is much safer to wear (i) ....

7 Underline or highlight five linking words in these two paragraphs.
8 Write a third paragraph for this essay, explaining what safety law you would introduce. Include one main idea and some supporting arguments, and link your ideas together well.

How can I improve my vocabulary range?

You have to know enough words to be accurate and avoid repetition. You can improve your vocabulary related to different topics by reading newspaper and magazine articles and noting some of the topic vocabulary.

1 Read the extract below in which the vocabulary related to task A on the left has been highlighted. What sort of publication do you think it comes from?

These days, noise and air pollution are serious environmental problems. Some people think that air travel is to blame. Others believe that we should reduce the number of vehicles on the roads.

Discuss both these views and give your opinion.

Environmentalists criticise many airlines because air travel contributes to global warming and also causes severe noise pollution around airports. Although jet engines are a lot quieter than they were fifteen years ago, there has been a huge increase in the number of flights, and so the noise level is high and constant for people living nearby.

To add to this, travellers are now criticising airlines for trying to squash too many people onto their planes. It is well documented that sitting on a plane for a considerable period of time is bad for your health. As a consequence, some airline companies are actually taking out a few rows of seats so that economy passengers have more space to move around in. This is a good idea but it will encourage more people to travel by plane, which will increase the amount of air traffic.

2 Complete the paragraphs below using some of the highlighted words or phrases.

These days, airlines are able to offer much cheaper **(a)** .... than in the past. This has led to an increase in the volume of **(b)** .... around the world's big **(c)** .... , which is good news for the **(d)** .... but not for the environment. As we all know, the more planes there are in the sky, the greater the chances are that **(e)** .... will increase.

Also, if you live near an airport, you have to put up with **(f)** .... from the engines, which is very stressful. However, as long as people want to travel, the **(g)** .... will continue to provide the service.

How important is accuracy?

You need to pay attention to how you choose, form and spell words. You will lose marks if you make mistakes in these areas.

3 Complete the gaps in these paragraphs with the correct form of the words in the box.

| decide |
| rough |
| quick |
| relax |
| scene |
| please |
| stress |
| fly |
| particular |
| air |
| fly |

If you need to make a decision about whether to drive or fly somewhere, you should consider (a) .... how much time you have for the journey. Obviously it is (b) .... to fly but it can be more (c) .... to drive, if you do not have to spend much time on busy roads. The (d) .... may also be a lot more interesting! Of course, driving can be quite an (e) .... experience during rush hour traffic and often it is just too (f) .... to even consider it.

The other factor to consider is the overall cost of (g) .... These days there are some very cheap deals available, (h) .... if you book well in advance. Low budget (i) .... are able to offer good prices for certain (j) .... that others cannot offer. If it is much cheaper to fly, you may prefer it.

▶▶▶▶▶▶▶▶▶▶▶▶▶▶▶▶

GRAMMAR

You need to show that you can write a range of sentence types and use grammar accurately. You also need to punctuate your writing well.

How can I show a range of sentence types?
You should include both simple and complex sentences in your essay. (Complex sentences contain more than one clause.)

Look at this paragraph from a student's essay. The sentences are all simple, so the examiner cannot give a high mark for grammar, even though the meaning is clear.

People have different opinions about the causes of noise and air pollution. I think their view depends on their personal circumstances. For example, it is very noisy near an airport. Some people live near airports. They want to reduce air travel. On the other hand, people live near busy roads. They argue that cars pollute the air. Cars give out too many fumes. Personally, I think both forms of transport are to blame.

Here is the same paragraph, re-written with a wider range of sentence types. This will get a better mark.

People have different opinions about the causes of noise and air pollution because of their personal circumstances. For example, if you live near an airport, you will hear a lot of noise every day. As a result, you may argue that air travel should be reduced. People who live near busy roads, however, might argue that it is cars that pollute the air by giving out too many fumes. Personally, I think both forms of transport are to blame.

How can I improve my accuracy?
It is important to know the typical mistakes that you make when you write. When you have finished writing, leave time to check your work for these.

1 Find the punctuation errors in this paragraph (there is one on each line).

dash after *relax*

a ....
b ....
c ....
d ....
e ....
f ....
g ....
h ....

Going on holiday should be fun and should help you relax you just need to be prepared. Some people dont manage to do this very well. If you go on a hiking holiday for example it is essential to take the right equipment with you otherwise you could be very uncomfortable. Similarly if you're staying in a hotel, its worth making sure there is a good public transport system nearby these are basic principles that can affect whether you return to work calm happy and refreshed or whether you are more stressed than you were when you left to go on holiday

ACTION PLAN

▶ Analyse the task to see if opposing views are expressed.
▶ Decide how many parts you have to write about.
▶ Decide on your position and your main ideas.
▶ Introduce your answer by re-phrasing the question and stating your position.
▶ Write three to five paragraphs that cover your main ideas and provide some supporting arguments.
▶ Link your ideas together so that your answer is logical and clearly developed.
▶ Try to use a range of relevant vocabulary and sentence types.
▶ Conclude by re-stating your position and summing up your arguments.
▶ Leave time to check your answer for errors. Look at spelling, grammar and punctuation.
▶ Count the number of words you have used.

ANSWERS PAGE 106
PRACTICE TEST PAGE 100

The Speaking Test

An 11–14-minute test of your ability to speak English

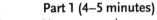

How many parts does the speaking test have?
The speaking test has three parts as follows:

Part 1 (4–5 minutes)
You answer short questions from the examiner about yourself and everyday situations.

Part 2 (3–4 minutes)
You give a one- to two-minute talk, based on your own experience, on a simple topic provided by the examiner.

Part 3 (4–5 minutes)
You discuss some general but more abstract topics with the examiner that are related to the Part 2 talk.

Why are there different parts to the speaking test?
The test aims to find out whether you can express yourself in English on a variety of personal, general and abstract topics, using informal and formal language.

What is the speaking test like?
The test takes place at the authorised test centre where you enrolled, usually on the day of the written test.

☐ ON THE DAY

- The speaking test usually takes place after the other parts of the test.

- Check your speaking test time and room with the administrator on the day.

- Take your passport (or photo identification as appropriate) with you so that you can show it to the examiner when he or she asks you. Take reading glasses, if you wear them. You do not need anything else.

- Arrive for the test early. You may be shown into a waiting room.

There is only one examiner and one candidate in each IELTS speaking test.

The examiner will record the test. Don't worry about this. The recording is used for administrative purposes.

All examiners are trained and regularly checked to ensure that they conduct the test reliably. You should not know the examiner.

What general approach should I take to the speaking test?
Follow the examiner's instructions and listen carefully. Make sure you speak clearly and answer only the questions that you are asked. The examiner will know if you have memorised answers and you will lose marks for this.

How is the speaking test marked?

The speaking test is marked using a 9-band scale, like all other parts of the test. The examiner will be listening to four features of your language: fluency and coherence, vocabulary, grammar and accuracy, and pronunciation.

Fluency and coherence **Can you keep talking?** Can you speak clearly and smoothly without a lot of hesitation? Can you link your ideas using a range of words and expressions?	**Grammar and accuracy** **Is your speech accurate?** Can you use different types of structure? Can the examiner understand you even if you make mistakes?
Vocabulary **Do you know enough appropriate words?** Can you talk about yourself and about less familiar topics? Do you know how to vary your words and expressions to fit the topic?	**Pronunciation** **Do you pronounce words correctly?** Can the examiner understand everything you say? Do you use intonation and stress appropriately?

Is each part of the test marked separately?

No. The examiner conducts the test and marks you according to your performance across all three parts of the test.

What if I don't understand the examiner?

You can ask him or her to repeat the question or explain a word, e.g.

> *Sorry, could you repeat the question, please?*

OR

> *Could you explain what ... means?*

If you still don't understand, let the examiner go on to the next question. You may get more confused if you ask for another repetition.

What if I'm not sure about the answer?

Remember that the speaking test is a language test NOT a test of your views or general knowledge. You can use expressions that give you some time to think about how you will answer a question.

> *I'm not sure what I think about ...*
> *Let me think ...*
> *I really don't know / can't remember.*
> *It depends on ...*
> *I tend to think that ...*
> *On the whole, it seems that ...*

When do I get my result?

The examiner is not allowed to tell you anything about your performance. You will get your result when you receive your Test Report Form. This is usually two weeks after you have taken the test.

The Test Report Form will show your scores for all four parts of the test (Listening, Reading, Writing and Speaking) and your overall Band Score.

Speaking Part 1

Part 1	Four to five minutes	General questions about everyday situations
Part 2	Three to four minutes	Short talk about a simple topic
Part 3	Four to five minutes	Discussion of abstract topics

What is the purpose of Part 1?
The examiner wants to hear you answer questions on a few simple topics to find out if you can talk about yourself and everyday situations. Talking about personal topics is usually easier than talking about more abstract topics.

1 Look at these two questions. Tick the one you think is a Part 1 question.
  a What do you like about travelling by train?
  b To what extent has air travel replaced train travel?

How will the test begin?
The examiner will begin with some introductory questions. You should answer these questions briefly and clearly.

ON THE DAY

- Wait to be called into the exam room.

- When you go into the exam room, the examiner will tell you where to sit.

- The examiner will introduce you on the recording. He or she will say your name, candidate number and the centre name.

The examiner will ask you to say your name and ask you where you come from.
He or she will then ask to see your passport or photo identification.
The examiner does not need a long reply to the introductory questions.

What will happen next?
The examiner will introduce the first Part 1 topic, which is always about your home town or your studies/work.

2 Answer these questions about your home town.

  a **What**'s your home town called?
  b **Where** is it?
  c **How long** have you lived there?
  d **Do you like** living there? Why?
  e **Is there anything you dislike about** your home town?

3 Think of some other questions you could be asked about your studies/work using the words in bold above to help you.

What other topics will the examiner cover in Part 1?

You may get questions on any general, everyday topic, so you need to have some ideas. Normally the examiner will ask a few questions on three topics in total and will introduce each new topic clearly. So once you have answered a few questions on one topic, be prepared for a change of topic.

4 Complete the topic boxes below by thinking of three more ideas for each box.

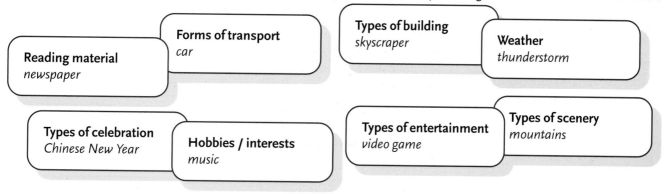

Reading material
newspaper

Forms of transport
car

Types of building
skyscraper

Weather
thunderstorm

Types of celebration
Chinese New Year

Hobbies / interests
music

Types of entertainment
video game

Types of scenery
mountains

How can I improve my range of topic vocabulary?

You can make topic banks like this:

Trains
fast / track / station / convenient / driver / speed / run

Mountains
peaceful / range / tall / snow-covered / climb / steep

and list phrases related to a topic like this:

Birthdays
an enjoyable celebration / giving presents

Languages
a useful skill / learning Chinese

5 Make some lists of words and phrases for the topic boxes in question 4 above.

6 Try to improve the way you describe things. Use one of these adjectives below in sentences a–i.

> impressive   depressing   enjoyable   complicated   relaxing
> informative   scary   sociable   tiring

a Some plane journeys are too long and ....
b The mountains near my home are high and very .... to look at.
c I learn from reading the newspaper because it's more .... than TV news.
d I find wet weather rather dull and ....
e Last year's Autumn Festival was a very .... occasion.
f The first time I went bungee jumping, it was pretty ....
g My uncle has lots of friends because he's a .... person.
h I prefer a .... holiday to an adventure holiday.
i I'm not very good at computer subjects because they seem so ....

7 Remember that words change their form depending on their use. Answer these questions using the correct form of the word in **bold**:

a Are you **prepared** for the test?
b How long does it take to **fly** to Mumbai?
c Is **pollution** a problem in Bangkok?
d Did the notes **help** you with the essay?
e Were you **free** to do as you liked at school?
f Do you dress for **comfort**?
g Do you play **golf**?
h Are there **crowds** of people on the trains?

a Yes, I've done lots of **preparation**.
b It's a seven-hour ....
c Yes, it's a very .... city.
d Yes, they were extremely ....
e No, we had very little ....
f Yes, I like wearing .... clothes.
g Yes, but I'm not a very good ....
h Yes, they're very ....

What sort of questions will the examiner ask?

The questions will be quite easy and will ask you to describe your likes and dislikes, your everyday life, your plans, etc. You may have to talk about the past, present or future and you may have to give simple opinions.

8 Look at the questions below on the topic of holidays. Which question
   a asks about your likes/dislikes?
   b asks you about your personal preferences?
   c requires a past tense answer?
   d invites you to suggest reasons?
   e asks you how regularly you do something?
   f asks you to give a general view on the topic?
   g asks you to give an account?

A **How often** do you go on holiday?

B **How do you prefer** to travel when you go on holiday?

C **What do you enjoy doing** when you're on holiday?

D **Why do you think** people need to go on holiday?

E **Tell me about** your last holiday.

How long should my answers be?

In Part 1, your answers should not be very long, but try to give a full answer. You need to show that you can keep talking, without too much hesitation, and that you can link your ideas together. The examiner cannot give you high marks if your responses are always very short. Here is an example of a short answer and a good answer.

How often do you go on holiday?

Twice a year, usually.

I usually go on holiday twice a year **but sometimes** I can only go once during the year **because** we are so busy at work. **So** it depends, really.

9 Go back to question 8 and try to answer the questions there by giving a full response.

What if I can't think of anything to say?
Remember that Part 1 is about you. Draw on your own experience, and don't be afraid to say how you feel about something.

How can I improve my accuracy?
Listen carefully to the question, which will help you decide what tenses to use and how to form your answer. Here is an example of a past tense question and answer.

> How old were you when you left school?

> I **was** only 15 when I **left** my high school but I **went** back to college two years later.

10 Answer these questions using the correct tense and, where appropriate, try to give a full answer.

> **a** What's your favourite subject?
> **b** Where did you first learn English?
> **c** Do you prefer being taught in a small or a big class?
> **d** Are you planning to do any exams in the near future?
> **e** Have you ever been in a school play?
> **f** Has your government made any recent changes in schools?

11 Find the errors in these answers and correct them.

> **a** Where do you come from?
> **b** How do you spend your leisure time?
> **c** Are you interested in fashion?
> **d** Do you live with your family or with friends?
> **e** What do you find difficult about learning English?
> **f** What do you enjoy about your course?
> **g** What are your plans for next year?
> **h** When do people in your country take holidays?
> **i** Do you like fruit?

> **a** I came from Tokyo.
> **b** I will play basketball.
> **c** Yes. I'm like fashion very much.
> **d** I'm living with my family since I'm born.
> **e** I am not easy to pronounce English words.
> **f** I enjoy discussing about economics.
> **g** I'm thinking to go to America.
> **h** Most of people go away in the summer.
> **i** I don't eat many fruit.

ACTION PLAN

▶ Respond briefly to the introductory questions.
▶ Make sure you can talk about your home town and your studies or work.
▶ Build some lists of phrases and topic banks.
▶ Listen to the question forms and the words that the examiner uses. These will help you form your answer.
▶ Try to give a full answer. The examiner wants to listen to you speak, so remember: it is important to talk.
▶ Don't memorise long answers. You will lose marks for this.
▶ Answer each question directly. Don't talk about something unrelated to the examiner's question.

✂ **ANSWERS PAGE 107**
PRACTICE TEST PAGE 101

Speaking Part 2

Part 1	Four to five minutes	General questions about everyday situations
Part 2	**Three to four minutes**	**Short talk about a simple topic**
Part 3	Four to five minutes	Discussion of abstract topics

What is the purpose of Part 2?

The examiner wants to hear you give a short talk about a simple topic based on your own experience, to see whether you can speak for one to two minutes on your own.

When does Part 2 begin?

When you have answered the last question in Part 1, the examiner will introduce Part 2.

The examiner will introduce Part 2 by saying: *Now, I'm going to give you a topic and I'd like you to talk about it for one to two minutes.*

Then the examiner will give you a piece of paper and a pen or pencil to make notes, and your topic. You will have one minute to prepare your talk.

Do I need to time myself in the test?

No. The examiner will time all the parts of the test. When you do the Part 2 talk, he or she will stop you when you have talked for a maximum of two minutes. However, you do need to have an idea of how long two minutes is, so that you can plan your talk.

What does the Part 2 topic look like?

The text will clearly state the topic that you need to talk about and will give some points to guide your talk.

The box on the left is an example of a topic.

1 Underline the topic, and the points that you need to cover in your talk.

What if I don't understand some of the words in the topic?

You can ask the examiner to explain any words you don't understand.

Describe a scientific development that has benefited mankind.

You should say:
what type of development it is
why it was needed
how it has been used

and explain why this scientific development was so beneficial.

How long will I have to make notes?

The examiner will give you one minute to make some notes. During this time, he or she will not talk to you. The notes are not marked and will be thrown away after the test. You cannot take them out of the room.

What if I haven't got any experience of the topic?
Use your imagination and invent some ideas. Remember that the examiner is testing your ability to speak English, not your views or general knowledge.

2 Here are six possible topics. Take two minutes to read through topics A–F and write down two ideas from your own experience for each one.
 A An activity that you enjoy.
 B An exciting experience from your childhood.
 C A person that you would like to meet.
 D A celebration that took place in your home town.
 E A job that you have done.
 F A play or concert that you have been in.

How can I make sure I choose a good idea to talk about?
The three points often begin with *How* or *Wh-* question words such as *why, who, when, whether, what* or *which*. These points are given to help you.

3 Read the topic in the box on the left and the start of the student's talk. What mistake has he made?

> Describe a plan you have made for your future that is not related to your studies.
>
> You should say:
>   what the plan is
>   when you think you will do it
>   how it could change your life
>
> and explain why you have made this plan.

I think I'll talk about getting married – that'll be easy.

I'm going to talk about my plan to get married. Er, I want to get married before I'm 30... Er, it'll change my life, obviously, er, because I won't be single any more... Er, I can't think...

4 Think of two plans you could talk about. Take about one minute to make an idea map, like the one below, for each plan.

What the plan is	
Buying a new guitar ⟶	• *mine's ten years old* • *it's my favourite pastime* • *there's a model I really like*

When you think you will do it	
Next year ⟶	• *I'll have more time and money next year* • *I need to concentrate on my studies now* • *I'll be 21 next year – a special birthday*

How it could change your life	
More opportunities ⟶	• *join a band* • *play better on a new instrument* • *impress my girlfriend*

5 Which of your plans do you think will be easier to talk about? Why?

Should I talk about the points in order?

You can cover the points in any order. You may have more to say about some points than others. This doesn't matter.

What tense should I speak in?

This will depend on the instructions. The tense may change through your talk depending on the points you are given.

6 Underline or highlight all the different verb tenses in the talk below on 'an activity that you enjoy'.

> *I enjoy doing Taekwondo because I've always been interested in martial arts. Even when I was a little kid I used to watch films and dream of getting my black belt. So I had my first class at the age of seven. Most of the other students were older than me. Nowadays, I have less time but I still try to go to classes at least once a month.*

7 What points do you think the student was given to talk about?

How should I start my talk?

When the minute's preparation time is over, the examiner will tell you to begin. Your opening words should tell the examiner what you have chosen to talk about.

8 Fill in the gaps in the talks below using an appropriate verb in an appropriate tense. You can use more than one word for each space and choose your own verbs. Then read the talks aloud.

> **A** *I'm going to talk about my first job.*
> *I .... in a small village in the countryside, but soon after that, my family moved to Bangkok and I .... there until I .... my studies. I got used to the big city so after that I .... abroad to work for a multinational company. This job ....*

> **B** *The person I'd like to meet is the president of our country because he .... a very important person. He's .... by the people and .... in office for five years. I think it .... an honour to meet him and I .... very proud.*

> **C** *I'd like to talk about the royal wedding that took place in Copenhagen in 2004. The Prince of Denmark .... married to a young woman from Australia, and I .... lucky enough to be in Copenhagen at the time of the wedding. Thousands of people .... out onto the streets to watch the couple go past in an open carriage. Even though I .... believe in fairy tales, this .... a real fairy-tale wedding.*

How can I show a range of topic vocabulary?

Make a mind map of some of the vocabulary and ideas you can use. The examiner will be listening to see whether you know a range of words related to the topic. Use as many as you can and don't worry too much about making mistakes. Imagine this is your topic.

Describe an adventure from your childhood.

You should say:
  where you were
  who you were with
  what happened

and explain why you think it was an adventure.

I think I'll talk about when I was rescued by a helicopter… hiking with friends… broke my ankle… yes… good idea!

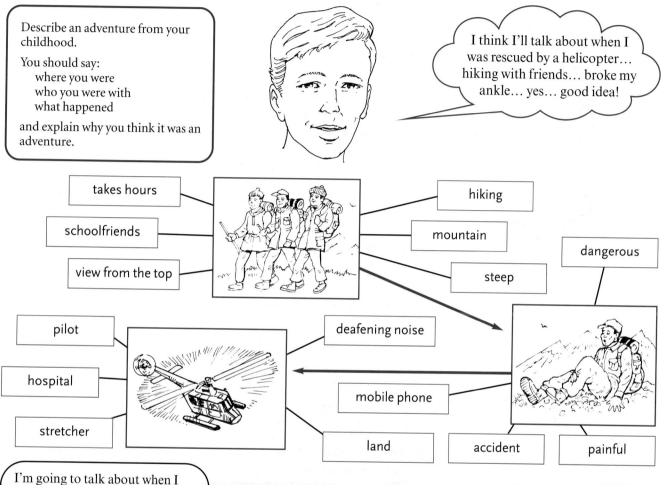

takes hours

schoolfriends

view from the top

hiking

mountain

steep

dangerous

pilot

hospital

stretcher

deafening noise

mobile phone

land

accident

painful

I'm going to talk about when I went **(a)** …….. with some of my **(b)** …….. in the French Alps. Er, it was a school holiday and so we decided to climb a famous **(c)** …….. called La Tournette. It's not difficult but it **(d)** …….. to get up to the top and there are a couple of places where it's rather **(e)** …….. . But it's worth it because the **(f)** …….. is incredible. Even in warm weather, you can find snow there, too.

9 Use some of the words in the mind map to complete the first part of the student's talk on the left.

ACTION PLAN

▶ Read the whole topic carefully first.
▶ Choose an idea that you can talk about for up to two minutes.
▶ Think about the tenses you will use.
▶ Prepare some ideas for the whole talk, not just the opening.
▶ Don't talk about something unrelated to the topic.
▶ Introduce your topic clearly at the start of your talk.

ANSWERS PAGE 108
PRACTICE TEST PAGE 101

Speaking Part 3

Part 1	Four to five minutes	General questions about everyday situations
Part 2	Three to four minutes	Short talk about a simple topic
Part 3	**Four to five minutes**	**Discussion of abstract topics**

What is the purpose of Part 3?

The examiner wants to hear you discuss some general but more abstract topics that are related to the Part 2 talk.

When does Part 3 begin?

At the end of your two-minute talk, the examiner will lead you into Part 3 by asking you about a more general aspect of the topic.

🗋 ON THE DAY

- The examiner will ask you to give back the task when you have finished your talk.

- The examiner will always make the link between Parts 2 and 3, so you don't need to worry about this.

- Listen carefully to the first Part 3 question.

- If you do not understand a Part 3 question, the examiner can re-phrase it for you.

The examiner may ask a quick question on your Part 2 talk, e.g. *Have you always wanted to visit this place?* You need only give a short *Yes* or *No* answer. He or she will then introduce the Part 3 discussion by referring back to your Part 2 talk, e.g. *We've been talking about a place you'd like to visit and I'd like to discuss with you one or two more general questions related to this.*

What is an abstract topic?

How much time you spend watching television is about you and is a Part 1 topic. *Whether television has a negative effect on people* is more general and abstract and is a Part 3 topic.

1 Which of the following topics are Part 3 topics?
   a the impact of technology on work
   b your favourite newspaper
   c the effects of modern farming methods
   d teenage attitudes to parents
   e how you keep fit
   f whether competition is a positive thing
   g how your family celebrates Chinese New Year
   h why some children's stories are popular

What sort of questions will the examiner ask?

The examiner will ask a range of questions based on the topic from Part 2. The first question often asks you to describe or outline your views on a general aspect of this topic.

The examiner may begin with a question like this.

In your view, what are some of the benefits of travelling to new places?

The personal topic of 'a place I'd like to visit' has become a more general topic about travel. This is the sort of change I should expect in Part 3.

2 What are the key words in the question?

3 What could the student do to improve this response?

For a start, it can be very exciting, and it can also be personally rewarding.

If you give a short reply, the examiner will ask more questions to help you develop your answer. He or she may stress some words to help you.

What would you find **particularly** exciting about going to a new country?

In what way is it personally rewarding?

What strategy can I use to produce a good answer?
You need to focus on the key words in the question, and produce two or three ideas which you can support.

4 Look at this exchange between an examiner and a student, who has not provided enough language for the examiner to make a judgement about their level.

Do older people learn as much from travelling as younger people?

Yes, of course they do. I think it's the same.

Here are some useful strategies for developing ideas. Use the words provided to help you build a better answer to the question above.

Think about what other people might believe.	*Even though some people .... I think ....*
Make a direct contrast or comparison.	*I tend to think that while young people, ... older people ....*
Use personal experience.	*It's hard to say, but in my experience .... and so I think ....*
Refer back in time.	*I think in the past it was true that .... but nowadays ....*
Refer to the media.	*Newspapers and other media suggest that young people don't .... but I'm not sure they're right ....*
Analyse the question.	*I think it depends on the type of person. If the young person is .... , then .... but if they are .... , then ....*
Agree or disagree.	*Generally I would say that they do, but there are young people who ....*

5 Here is a response to the question *Who else benefits from the fact that people like to travel?* Which key idea does the student develop?

> *I think there can be lots of benefits for everyone... benefits for the person travelling and also for the people who live there, because many countries rely on tourism and so it's good when lots of visitors come. It provides work for the local people.*

How does Part 3 progress?

The questions will become more difficult. You can improve your answers in Part 3 if you understand how the topic is being developed and what abstract ideas might be related to it. Here is an example of a model chain of questions, which an examiner might ask about a topic.

Part 2 topic	Part 3 ideas
An activity that you enjoy.	Leisure centres / the role of sport in society / global sporting events

> How important is it for people to have a hobby?

> Do you think that there is too much emphasis on sport in our society today?

> Do global sporting events, such as the Olympic Games, have a role in the 21st century?

6 Try to think of possible Part 3 ideas for these two topics.

Part 2 topic	Part 3 ideas
A job that you have done.	
A play or concert that you have been in.	

7 Write down a few questions that the examiner could ask you on these two topics. Try to make them progressively more difficult.

How long should my answers be?

The examiner can only assess what you say, so it's important to give a full and relevant answer, linking your ideas smoothly. This skill is known as fluency.

How can I improve my fluency?

When you give an opinion, try to back it up by giving a reason for it or by offering a second point of view. Here are some useful expressions for doing this.

For me .... is very important	because ....
I think	but I can understand that ....
I don't really think much of	On the other hand ....
It all depends	Personally I believe ....
Some people feel	But I actually think ....

8 Complete the following answers to the examiner's three questions on page 86.

> *For me, having a hobby is ....*
> *because ....*

> *Some people feel that sport is a waste of*
> *time because ....*
> *But I actually think ....*

> *I don't really think the Olympic Games*
> *are .... On the other hand, the FIFA World*
> *Cup is always fantastic. I really ....*

How can I improve my pronunciation score?

You should speak loudly enough for the examiner to hear you, and try to pronounce your words clearly. Pay attention to the way you emphasise words and syllables within words, and try not to speak in a monotonous voice.

How can I identify my pronunciation weaknesses?

You can record your answers to any of the speaking exercises in this book and ask a teacher or a native speaker of English to help you identify your problem areas.

ACTION PLAN

▶ Give a full answer to each question and take the initiative.
▶ Think about how topics can be developed so that you are ready to explore the questions you are asked.
▶ Answer each question directly. Don't talk about something unrelated to the examiner's question.
▶ Try to link your ideas, so that your speech flows well.

ANSWERS PAGE 108
PRACTICE TEST PAGE 102

Practice Test

LISTENING

SECTION 1   Questions 1–10

Questions 1–3
Choose **THREE** letters **B–H**.

Which **THREE** other activities does the customer want to do?

Example (A) visit family
        B save money
        C study geography
        D study English
        E do some winter sports
        F go sailing
        G join a walking tour
        H meet young people

Questions 4–7
Complete the form below.

Write **NO MORE THAN THREE WORDS AND/OR A NUMBER** for each answer.

```
━━━━━━━━━ CUSTOMER'S DETAILS ━━━━━━━━━

Name               Su Ming Lee ...........................
Address          4 ......... 8.9 .. Tech Street ..... Kew
Mobile           5 0402 ............................
Day and date
of departure     6 ......... Saturday .........
Length of course 7 ............................
Method of payment  credit card ........................
```

Questions 8–10
Label the map opposite.

Write the correct letter **A–G** next to questions 8–10.

8 The language school is at ......

9 The hotel is at ......

10 The bookshop is at ......

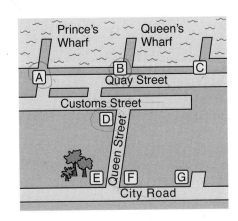

📄 **ANSWERS PAGE 109**
    RECORDING SCRIPTS PAGE 112

SECTION 2   Questions 11–20

Questions 11–13
Complete the sentences below.

*Write **NO MORE THAN THREE WORDS** for each answer.*

11 .....cities..... are often known by their famous bridges.

12 The speaker compares a bridge to a cathedral or ....

13 Sydney Harbour Bridge is nicknamed ....

Questions 14–18
Complete the table below.

*Write **NO MORE THAN THREE WORDS AND/OR A NUMBER** for each answer.*

Date	Event
1916	**14** .... agreed to finance bridge
15 ..1924..	Contract signed with engineering firm
1926	Construction involved: • knocking down **16** .... • creation of many jobs
1932	Bridge completed at a cost of **17** £ ....
March 1932	Opening ceremony Ribbon cut by a man riding a **18** ....

Questions 19–20
Answer the questions below.

*Write **NO MORE THAN THREE WORDS AND/OR A NUMBER** for each answer.*

19 How long is the tunnel?

....

20 Name **ONE** thing the tunnel can withstand.

....

⚷ **ANSWERS PAGE 109**
  RECORDING SCRIPTS PAGE 113

SECTION 3   Questions 21–30

Question 21
*Choose the correct letter **A**, **B** or **C**.*

21 Which graph shows the
distribution of animals painted
on the caves?

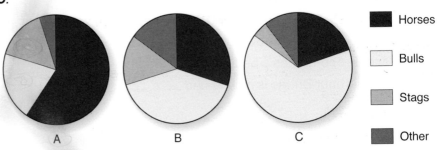

Questions 22–25
How does the woman describe each type of drawing?

*Choose your answers from the box and write the letters **A–H** next to questions 22–25.*

22 bulls   ....

23 humans   ....

24 signs   ....

25 fish   ....

A uncommon	**E** consisting of dots
B realistic	**F** complex
C two-dimensional	**G** important
D childish	**H** huge

Questions 26–27
Label the diagram below.

*Write **NO MORE THAN THREE WORDS** for each answer.*

26 ....

27 ....

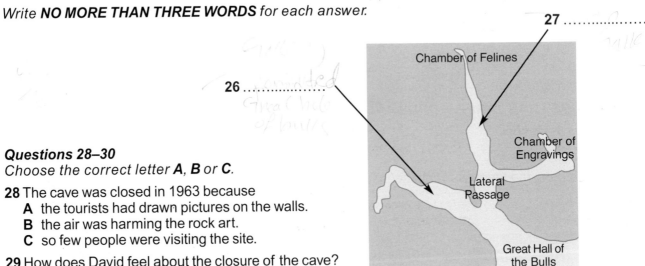

Questions 28–30
*Choose the correct letter **A**, **B** or **C**.*

28 The cave was closed in 1963 because
   A the tourists had drawn pictures on the walls.
   B the air was harming the rock art.
   C so few people were visiting the site.

29 How does David feel about the closure of the cave?
   A He agrees with the decision.
   B He thinks it was a bad idea.
   C He has no views on the matter.

30 How can people enjoy the drawings today?
   A The government has re-opened the cave.
   B The drawings have been photographed.
   C A replica of the cave has been built.

ANSWERS PAGE 109
RECORDING SCRIPTS PAGE 114

SECTION 4   Questions 31–40

Questions 31–32
Complete the notes below.

Write **NO MORE THAN THREE WORDS** *for each answer.*

What is marketing?

31 ………………….... and …………………… represent only two aspects of marketing.

Marketing involves

• finding customers

• ensuring customer satisfaction

• **32** …………………………………..

Questions 33–34
Complete the flow chart below.

Write **NO MORE THAN TWO WORDS** *for each answer.*

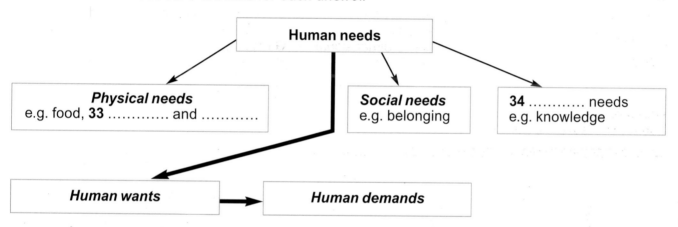

Questions 35–38
Which market research method is used by each of these businesses?

Write the correct letter **A–C** *next to questions 35–38.*

A customer observation	**35** supermarkets …………
B free offers	**36** department stores …………
C in-store surveys	**37** fast-food companies …………
	38 theme parks …………

Questions 39–40
Complete the notes below.

Write **NO MORE THAN THREE WORDS** *for each answer.*

Customer satisfaction

Product performance	Customers are
• poor	• unhappy
• good	• **39** …………………………
• **40** …………………………	• delighted

ANSWERS PAGE 109
RECORDING SCRIPTS PAGE 115

GENERAL TRAINING READING

SECTION 1   Questions 1–14

Questions 1–5
Look at the contents page below from a booklet on living in Australia.

Write the appropriate page numbers in boxes 1–5 on your answer sheet.

Which page should you refer to if you

1 need to help a grandparent travel to Australia for a holiday with you?
2 would like to know how old your son should be to learn to drive?
3 are having an argument with your landlord?
4 wish to enrol a relative on a carpentry course?
5 want to have your family's teeth checked?

Contents

What to do soon after arrival

Help with English

Emergency Services

Housing

Employment

Social Security

Transport

Education and Childcare

The Health System Medicare

Recreation and Media

Department of Immigration and Multicultural and Indigenous Affairs

Local Government and Community Service

Questions 6–10

Look at the information from a government website below.

Looking for Work • • • • • • • • • • • • • • • • • •

The daily newspapers advertise job vacancies, from Monday to Friday, and often provide a special in-depth section on work opportunities on Saturday. There are also private employment agencies, which are listed in the Yellow Pages telephone directory and internet employment boards.

Any Australian resident can register with Centrelink for help in finding a job. You need to do this if you want to be referred to Job Network, which consists of hundreds of private, community and government organisations, contracted to the Commonwealth Government to help people find employment.

As a newcomer, it is often a good idea to talk to an experienced employment counsellor to ensure that your approach to job-seeking is appropriate, particularly if you are having difficulty getting an interview.

Job Network Services

There are a number of employment services available under the Job Network. These include:

- Intensive Support Services – provide further assistance to eligible job seekers including training them to develop interview skills, and to be able to present themselves well to potential employers.

- Intensive Support – customised assistance – provides more one-to-one help to eligible job seekers, and includes addressing a job seeker's barriers to employment and tailors the job seeker's efforts in looking for work.

- The New Enterprise Incentive Scheme (NEIS) – helps unemployed people start and run their own business. Participants may be able to get NEIS assistance which provides small business training, income support and advice during the first year of business.

It is important to remember that just joining a Job Network provider does not guarantee a job. You still need to actively seek work to increase your chances of finding a job.

All job seekers can also use the free Job Network Access facilities at Centrelink and a number of Job Network Member Agencies. These include telephones, photocopiers, fax machines, touch screens and computers (including the internet).

Do the following statements agree with the information given in the passage?

In boxes 6–10 on your answer sheet, write

TRUE   *if the statement agrees with the information*
FALSE   *if the statement contradicts the information*
NOT GIVEN *if there is no information on this*

6 The best day to look in the newspaper for a job is Saturday.

7 You can use the Job Network without being registered with Centrelink.

8 Some employment counsellors are specially trained to deal with new residents.

9 It is best to contact one of the Intensive Support Services if you need financial help while setting up a company.

10 Job Network Agencies charge a small fee for use of their facilities.

Questions 11–14

Read the information below about a new fitness centre.

Complete the table below.

Choose **NO MORE THAN THREE WORDS** *from the passage for each answer.*

Write your answers in boxes 11–14 on your answer sheet.

℘ FITNESS CENTRE ℘

The fitness centre offers a variety of activities for members of all ages throughout the week.

Activities for Monday 12 July

Learn to swim Classes for pre-school children aged five and under start at 10 am. Classes last 30 minutes and parents must attend with their children. Don't forget to book, as places are limited, and to pack some warm clothes for after the lesson.

Women's aerobics Sessions are for one hour and begin at 10.45 am, led by Melissa. Come along and join us every Monday for an exhilarating hour of exercise and fun. Leave your kids at the nursery and take time out for yourself. Wear a track suit or something similar.

Lunchtime yoga Take a break at lunchtime (1.00 – 2.00 pm) for an hour of meditation and yoga. Enjoy the peace and quiet of our meditation room, and relaxing sessions designed for active people with busy lives. Use your own mat for floor work or hire one from us for a small sum.

Activity	Starting time	Need to bring
pre-school swimming	10.00 am	**11** ......
12	10.45 am	track suit
yoga	**13**	**14** ......

SECTION 2   Questions 15–20

Questions 15–20

The extract from the Oxford Tutorial College website has six paragraphs **A–F**.

Choose the correct heading for each paragraph from the list of headings below.

*Write the correct number **i–ix** in boxes 15–20 on your answer sheet.*

List of Headings
i Am I a suitable student for this course?
ii What will I gain from studying Film Studies?
iii How will I be assessed?
iv What is covered in Film Studies?
v What happens if I fail?
vi How is the course divided up?
vii Who runs the course?
viii What do I need to purchase for the course?
ix How long is the course?

15 Paragraph **A**
16 Paragraph **B**
17 Paragraph **C**
18 Paragraph **D**
19 Paragraph **E**
20 Paragraph **F**

Oxford Tutorial College

A 'A' Level Film Studies specifications are designed to deepen students' understanding, appreciation and enjoyment of film. A wide range of films is studied and students are encouraged to explore the artistic, cultural and economic meanings produced by the form. Film Studies combines well with a variety of other subjects, including Modern Languages, Art and Design and Art History.

B The emphasis is on visual storytelling and audience response. As such, the course develops skills of observation, critical analysis and personal reflection, which may be taken forward into degree courses for arts, humanities, media and related fields. Film Studies 'A' level also provides a strong base for progression to undergraduate studies in Film Theory, Film Criticism and Film History.

C Students of Film Studies are not required to have completed a GCSE in a related subject prior to undertaking 'A' level, though a grade C or better in English Language is recommended. Some experience of textual analysis such as in literature or humanities would be very helpful, particularly if the student aims to complete the course in one year. Prospective students of this subject should certainly have an interest in a broad range of films, including non-Hollywood films.

D The course tutor is Andrew Hogan, who is a Media Studies graduate of Luton University. His life-long passion for film has led him into teaching, and into a variety of film-related jobs, most notably as education officer for the Oxford arthouse cinema The Phoenix Picture House. He is currently teaching himself 16mm cinematography and attempting to watch at least two new films a day.

E Students wishing to re-take Film Studies can do so over a year with the exam being taken in June. Time is taken to consolidate and improve on knowledge and skills which were lacking the first time round. Where the modular results have been uneven, the better marks can be retained, with concentration focused solely on those modules in which the candidate under-performed.

F Film Studies is normally structured to combine small seminar groups with individual tuition. The induction period develops students' own understanding of their experience as film viewers. The relationship between spectator and film underpins the approach to cinema for this specification. Students normally attend four group seminars a week and also receive one hour of individual tuition per week to support group discussions and independent work required by the coursework units.

This page was last changed on 17 December 2004 | ©2004 Oxford Tutorial College Ltd

Questions 21–27

Read the newspaper review below of private adult education centres.

What's on offer in the private sector

••

Jenny Harrison reports

Not all schools can offer the range of courses and expertise that is available at Parish Court. In addition to the highly motivated staff, they also have an impressive range of resources that should suit all those interested in updating their IT skills. Located in a 16th century farmhouse in the heart of the Suffolk countryside, the surroundings offer ample quiet for study periods. All courses are residential so be prepared to pay!

If you live a busy, hectic lifestyle, you will appreciate the possibility of attending the course of your choice, without adding to your daily travel programme. Harvard Benn Centre is only a five-minute walk from the mainline station and so is within easy access to students, even if they live outside the town. The offices cover four floors of the building and have been brought up to date following a year-long refurbishment plan. A recent hike in fees has followed, though.

At James Cattan the suite of purpose-built classrooms which provide all kinds of up-to-the-minute facilities are impressive. Situated in a prize section of Lakeland Science Park, they pride themselves on being one of the first adult education centres in the area to be able to promote the fact that they fully cater for students with mobility problems and the good parking facilities might also tempt those who choose not to walk from the city bus terminal. All this for quite reasonable course rates.

Be prepared to walk right past ICE. The rather modest identification outside the building amounts to little more than a small board in the Victorian window. However, once inside, all feelings of doubt are removed by the bustling energy of the staff and the lively interior. Classrooms and courses are well signposted and if you don't know where to go, there is always someone there to lend a hand. Fees are standard.

It's an unusual name for a school but Romeo's Institute aims to lure you into their educational extravaganza with brightly-coloured furniture, high-tech gadgetry and a trendy restaurant. So far so good, but do the quality of the staff and what's on offer match the external surroundings? The answer is 'yes' and 'no'. They teach a few courses well but it would benefit from having a little more on offer. Fees could also be lower.

Questions 21–27

Look at the following statements (questions 21–27) and the list of Centres below.

Match each statement with the correct centre A–E.

Write the correct letter A–E in boxes 21–27 on your answer sheet.

21 Prices have just risen.
22 It would suit a wheelchair user.
23 The number of subjects on offer is limited.
24 It enjoys a rural setting.
25 First impressions can be off-putting.
26 It has been recently modernised.
27 It offers value for money.

List of Centres

A Parish Court
B Harvard Benn Centre
C James Cattan
D ICE
E Romeo's Institute

SECTION 3 Questions 28–40

Read the passage below and answer questions 28–40.

Mary had a little gramophone

*Edison's 'talking machine' turned music from a
performing art into a recording industry*

Music has always existed but until the late 19th century it could not be caught. It could not be tamed or owned. It belonged to the air. Then on December 6 1877, Thomas Edison finished the first prototype of his talking machine, a device that could record the human voice onto a tin foil roll and play it back in scratchy low fidelity. Edison chose as his test material the words of a nursery rhyme *Mary had a little lamb*, speaking them into the horn of his memory machine. What the inventor thought he had created was a tool, which would allow us access to the past, to make and listen to 'records' of past events and achievements in the archival sense of the word.

But inventions are rarely used as they are intended, and Edison's would, within decades, leave its spoken word intentions behind and fundamentally alter the role of music in society. Edison's phonograph would turn sound into an artefact, as well as an experience. Though its effects would be far-reaching, it took decades for the phonograph to transcend its beginning as an electrical curiosity. This was partly because the reproduction quality of early machines was so low and partly because Edison, being a little deaf, was not very interested in using it for musical purposes.

But others began to sense the phonograph's true value. The first piece of music composed specifically for recording was in 1904 and within two decades, composers as famous as Stravinsky were writing for recording rather than for performance. By the middle of the century, in popular music at least, the record had become the object, and the performance a secondary reproduction of it.

The most significant turning point, however, came not on the creative side, but on the consumer one. In 1906, the Victor company released the first phonograph designed as a piece of household furniture, in 'piano-finished' mahogany. It retailed for $US 200. Until this point, record players had existed mostly in public places, in the cafés of Europe and the saloons of America. The spread of the record player would have an effect on music similar to that of the Gutenberg printing press on the written word. It would democratise music, making it intersect with the everyday lives of ordinary people.

The previous two centuries had already seen a move away from the dominance of ceremonial and ritual music (written for public events or religious needs) towards the realm of pure art, music for its own sake as expressed by the likes of Mozart and Beethoven. The record player would force music to go further, to answer the needs of daily life, to become entertainer, informer and friend, to provide joy, calm and energy, to furnish everything from ambience for airport lounges to identity for teenagers.

In doing this, it would reverse a power relationship that had existed since music's first note. In the post-phonograph world, the listener has the power to decide what to listen to, when to listen to it and where to listen. Until the record, the ways in which music could be approached were prescribed by others. But the phonograph changed all this.

Recorded music was also boosted by the spread of radio in the first half of the 20th century which brought music into the homes of ordinary people. The next significant milestone was the introduction of magnetic tape in the late 1940s which changed the concept of how music could be made. Until this point, records had been based on the notion of 'bottled' live performance. Magnetic tape allowed disparate pieces to be edited together.

About the same time, the vinyl record replaced the breakable shellac, with the 78 rpm giving way to the $33^1/_3$ rpm record for classical works and popular albums, and a smaller version for singles. These formats, which coincided with the rock explosion, lasted only three decades, phased out after the arrival of the CD in the mid-1980s. Multi-track recording popularised in the 1960s continued music's move away from 'performance' and allowed instruments and vocals to be recorded separately and spliced together, creating room for overdubs of musical and vocal parts, and making it easy to fix bad notes or piece together elements to create an illusion of the whole.

More recently, an even greater leap has been brought about by the invention of digital recording tools. Today's music is recorded on equipment that did not even exist a generation ago. Computers mean that 'recordings' can now be made without a microphone, without tape and without anything recognisable as an instrument to anyone over the age of 35. A significant amount of popular music is no longer written, but constructed. This technique, often referred to as sampling, has allowed composition to become a process of appropriation and re-contextualisation.

The recording methods of the early 20th century, as revolutionary as they were, now seem imbued with simple, traditional, almost rustic virtue. It is no longer necessary to be able to read music or play any kind of instrument to put together a song. Anyone can push a button on a drum machine. Anyone can recycle a great guitar riff or flute loop from an old 45. Some see this as desecration. Others see it as a triumph. It may well be both. More likely it's just the opening notes of a symphony we can't even imagine yet.

Questions 28–32
Do the following statements agree with the views of the writer in Reading Passage 3?

In boxes 28–32 on your answer sheet, write

YES   *if the statement agrees with the views of the writer*
NO   *if the statement contradicts the views of the writer*
NOT GIVEN   *if it is impossible to say what the writer thinks about this*

28 Edison created his talking machine to record history.

29 The invention of the phonograph immediately changed the way in which society related to music.

30 Stravinsky disliked having to perform his compositions in public.

31 The record player influenced music more than the printing press influenced the written word.

32 In the 17th and 18th centuries, music became an art form in its own right.

Questions 33–37
*Complete each sentence with the correct ending **A–H** below.*

*Write the correct letter **A–H** in boxes 33–37 on your answer sheet.*

33 People were able to control what they listened to with

34 Early 20th century recorded music grew in popularity with

35 By the 1940s the emphasis on recording live performances had become outdated thanks to

36 The enormous growth in rock music occurred at the same time as

37 By the 1960s recording errors could be repaired due to

A the growth of cafés in Europe.	**E** the democratisation of music.
B the creation of magnetic tape.	**F** the innovation of multi-track recording techniques.
C the widespread introduction of the record player.	
D the introduction of vinyl records.	**G** the expansion of radio.
	H the arrival of the compact disc.

Questions 38–40
Complete the summary below.

*Choose **ONE WORD** from the passage for each answer.*

Write your answers in boxes 38–40 on your answer sheet.

Digital Recording
Many contemporary recordings today are created using computers and it is no longer necessary to use a microphone or a conventional **38** .... . Music is constructed using material from previous recordings. This is known as **39** .... . Some people disapprove of this approach, while others consider it to be a **40** .... or possibly a combination of the two.

⊶ ANSWERS PAGE 109

GENERAL TRAINING WRITING

WRITING TASK 1

You should spend about 20 minutes on this task.

> *A friend you met last year has invited you to visit them in their country. You have never been there before and need some information before you leave.*
>
> *Write a letter to your friend. In your letter*

- *request advice about a gift for his/her family*
- *ask about activities and clothing*
- *find out about the food*

Write at least 150 words.

You do **NOT** need to write any addresses.

Begin your letter as follows:

Dear ……………..

⚷ *Read the sample answer on page 109 and go through the checklist.*

	✔	Comments
Is the letter in the correct style?		
Does the letter begin and end in the correct way?		
Can you underline the purpose?		
Can you underline the main ideas?		
Are the paragraph breaks in the right place?		
Can you identify the linkers and reference words?		
Can you identify the topic vocabulary?		
Is there a range of structures?		
Is the letter long enough?		

WRITING TASK 2

You should spend about 40 minutes on this task.

Write about the following topic:

> ***Some people think that it is important to use leisure time for activities that improve the mind, such as reading and doing word puzzles. Other people feel that it is important to rest the mind during leisure time.***
>
> ***Discuss both these views and give your opinion.***

Give reasons for your answer and include any relevant examples from your own knowledge or experience.

Write at least 250 words.

Read the sample answer on page 110 and go through the checklist.

	✓	Comments
Can you identify the writer's position?		
Can you underline the main ideas in each paragraph?		
Can you identify the linkers and reference words?		
Can you identify the topic vocabulary?		
Can you find a range of sentence types?		
Is the answer long enough?		

SPEAKING

PART 1

1 Now, in this first part, I'd like to ask you some questions about yourself. Let's talk about your work. Where do you work?
Do you enjoy your work? Why / Why not?
What kinds of tasks do you have to do at work?
Have you ever been late for work?
Why / Why not?

2 I'd like to move on now to talk about fashion.
Tell me about the popular clothes and fashions in your country.
What sort of fashion shops do you have in your country?
Have fashions changed very much since you were younger?
Is it important for you to be in fashion? Why / Why not?

3 Let's move on to the topic of the internet.
How often do you use the internet?
Does everyone in your family use the internet?
What do you use the internet for?
When did you last use the internet?

If you have someone to study with, take it in turns to ask and answer the questions.

((◖ Listen to the sample on the recording and complete the checklist. (CD Track 16)

	✔	Comments
Did the student directly answer the questions?		
Did he use a range of words?		
Did he link his ideas together well?		
Did he say enough?		
Were the answers easy to understand?		

PART 2

Describe a place that you would like to visit.

You should say:
where it is
when you would like to go there
who you would like to go with

and explain why you would like to visit this place.

1 Now, I'm going to give you a topic, and I'd like you to talk about it for one to two minutes.
Before you talk, you'll have one minute to think about what you're going to say.
You can make some notes if you wish. Do you understand?
Here's some paper and a pencil, for making notes, and here's your topic.

If you have someone to study with, take it in turns to do the talk in one to two minutes.

((◖ Listen to the sample on the recording and complete the checklist. (CD Track 17)

	✔	Comments
Did the student talk for two minutes?		
Did he stick to the topic?		
Did he cover the three main points?		
Did the talk flow well?		
Did he use a range of words?		

2 All right?
Remember you have one to two minutes for this, so don't worry if I stop you. I'll tell you when the time is up. Can you start speaking now, please?

⚷ **ANSWERS PAGE 110**

PART 3

1 We've been talking about a place you'd like to visit and I'd like to discuss with you one or two more general questions related to this.

So, let's consider first of all the idea, as a student, of having a gap year.

2 How important do you think it is for young people to visit different places before they go to university or college? What sort of challenges do you think you'd have, going on a gap year as a student? Do you think it's useful to work, for other reasons as well, besides money? What sort of jobs do you think would be the best sort of jobs to do? What sort of preparation should a student make before they go on a gap year, do you think?

3 OK. Let's move on to the topic of travelling to less familiar places. What sort of advantages are there to reading about a country before you visit it? Do you think there are any disadvantages? Some people choose to have a guide, when they go to a very unfamiliar place. Do you think that improves the quality of a travel experience? Do you think you learn more from visiting important sites or from meeting local people?

If you have someone to study with, take it in turns to ask and answer the questions.

((► Listen to the sample recording and complete the checklist. (CD Track 18)

	✔	Comments
Did the student respond to the key ideas?		
Did the student support his answers well?		
Did he use a range of words?		
Did he speak fluently, using a range of linkers?		

☞ **ANSWERS PAGE 110**

Answer Key

Listening Section 1

1 a, c, f, h

Pick from a list

2 identification / passport
study English / learn a language
fly / go by plane
building / house
painting / picture
headgear / helmet
vehicle / car
meal / lunch
bag / suitcase
thunderstorm / wet weather
winter sports / skiing

3 and **4** C, E (in any order)

Form filling

5 NB Answers provide examples of how these times and
dates are said, not written.
Seven fifty / Ten to eight (in the morning)
Six forty-five / A quarter to seven (in the morning)
Ten fifteen / A quarter past ten (in the morning)
One am / One o'clock (in the morning)
Thirteen hundred hours / One pm / One o'clock (in the
afternoon)

6 The twenty-first of November / November the twenty-first
The twenty-fourth of March / March the twenty-fourth
The twenty-second of December / December the twenty-
second
The eighteenth of August / August the eighteenth

7 a a name **b** a date with a year **c** a family name
d a condition / an illness

8 C A R O L I N E Black

9 22 November 1984 / 22nd November 1984 / November
22nd 1984 / November 22 1984

10 129 807

11 Ford station wagon

Labelling a map or plan

12 Queen Victoria Building

13 Bottom right-hand corner

14 Market Street, Martin Place, Hunter Street, Bridge Street

15 The Opera House

16 Queen Victoria Building / QVB

17 department store

18 hotel

19 library

Listening Section 2

1 A Pavilion / built 1784 / re-built 1815–1820 / Indian and
Chinese styles

B koala park / zoo
koalas popular / loveable appearance but long claws /
be careful

Sentence/summary completion

2 a a noun (form of transport)
b a noun (animal or plant)
c a number (date/period)
d a noun (material)
e an adjective (positive)
f an adjective (negative)

3 200 years / two hundred years

4 (white) stone

5 under (the) waves/water / underwater

6 summer months / summer

7 It is OK to use words or figures here.

Table completion

8 comparing 3 hotels: key words are rate / rate includes /
facilities

9 A a service **B** $ amount and a service **C** a facility

10 11.15 am (must have *am* or *morning*)

11 *The Long Journey*

12 (classic) action (film)

Short answer questions

13 a When / restaurant *Time or date*
b Where / paintings *Place: building or city*
c How many / concert *Number*
d Why / telephone *Reason*
e What / man's bag *Item/thing = noun*
f Who / party *Person or name*
g What / old lady *Event or incident*
h How / hurt *Explanation*

14 ground floor

15 photography / photographs

16 films / lectures / concerts

17 Q16 must have two pieces of information to get one mark.

Listening Section 3

1 B A C

2 C B A D

3 Set 1 – Speaker C; Set 2 – Speaker B

4 Set 1 – Speaker B; Set 2 – Speakers B and D

5 A iii **B** i

6 A no **B** yes **C** no

Multiple choice

7 C

8 Possible re-phrasing of the three options.
A To protect them from illness.
B To provide them with extra food.
C So that they stay pink in colour.

9 Option A: flamingo health is not mentioned on the
recording, so option A is not correct. Option B: food and
diet are mentioned on the recording, but the speaker says
not getting enough food was not the problem, so option B
is not correct.

Matching

10 B played in many countries / popular all over the world
    C could be harmful / could hurt yourself
    D lots of people play this
    E the things you need to play cost a lot of money
    F not difficult to learn
    G fun to look at / good spectator sport
11 E
12 B
13 F
14 C
15 if it included some more examples / usually pretty good / groundbreaking / very high standard / hasn't been assessed yet

Labelling a diagram

16 C
17 D
18 E

Listening Section 4

1 1 f 2 c 3 a 4 b 5 d 6 e 7 g 8 h 9 j 10 i
2 A In fact / Surprisingly enough (2/4)
    B On the other hand (10)
    C One way (1)
    D lastly (6)
    E generally speaking (8)
    F surprisingly enough / in fact / generally speaking (4/2/8)

Note completion

3 The topic is science/DNA.
    What does a string of DNA look like?
    What two things does DNA have something in common with?
4 an object / something biological
5 ball of string
6 other animals / plants
7 Australia
8 marketing strategies
9 TV programme

Flow chart completion

10 by hand
11 mills
12 labelled
13 at home / abroad
14 the first step is to / after this initial process / incidentally / then / finally

Classification

15 waste disposal methods
16 ways of disposing of different materials
17 C **18** C **19** A **20** A **21** B

General Training Reading Section 1

Short answer questions

1 –   Hove
2 number / letters   BN3 2EG
3 a phone number   01273 290700
4 a day   Tuesday
5 a group of people   disabled drivers
6

1	Church Rd. Hove	too many words
2	BN3 2GE	incorrect sequence
3	290700	incomplete number
4	Teusday	spelling mistake
5	disabled driver	's' missing on *driver*

True / False / Not Given

7 T **8** T **9** F **10** NG **11** F

Sentence completion

12 an adjective
13 a number
14 two nouns
15 20th century
16 athletics
17 books

Notes / table / flow chart completion

18 passport
19 Form 601
20 (supporting) documents
21 Immigration Office
22 stamped addressed

Labelling a diagram

23 diving board
24 (25-metre) (swimming) pool
25 squash courts
26 gymnasium
27 restaurant

General Training Reading Section 2

Paragraph headings

1 ii
2 The key words, topic sentence and vocabulary have been highlighted.
3 i and iii are attractive because the key words *applying* and *courses* are in the paragraph but there is no information given on either.
4 iv
5 ii
6 i
7 iii The word *safe* is in paragraph A but checking safety features is not the paragraph theme.
    v Paragraph C is about discussing facilities with the landlord, not the occupants.

Finding information in paragraphs

9 A

10 C

11 A

12

9 two ways / keeping schedule	list of tasks / electronic diary
10 recommendation / building world knowledge	what is going on around you / increase understanding / it's a good idea /everyday life / outside your course work
11 example / poor time management	morning / essay by lunchtime/ badly

Matching

13 D **14** C **15** C **16** A **17** B

Classification

19 B **20** C **21** B

Features	Course 1113	Course 1345	Answer
19 offers personalised training	✗	✓	B
20 is run at weekends	✓	✓	C
21 focuses on improving photography techniques	✗	✓	B

Multiple choice

22 D

23 B They get confused between what is a fact and what is an opinion.

C They need help understanding the language on some courses.

D They fail to take an objective view of study.

Pick from a list

24 and **25** C, E (in any order)

26 The phrases are *don't give up half way* and *come back to the trickier material and read that in more detail when you have time.*

General Training Reading Section 3

Yes / No / Not Given

1 a, c and e

2 Mostly the writer's opinion.

one of these is decidedly more glamorous than the other / this has overshadowed the less glamorous side of the industry / The people involved in digital security come across as bright and interesting, whereas the door-lock people do not. This second group soon have to admit that there have been no real advances in locks since the invention of the pin-tumbler lock

3 N **4** Y **5** NG **6** Y **7** NG **8** Y **9** N

10 *are standard fittings, as are remote locking systems for*

6Y *most new cars.*

7NG *guests are issued, not with a key, but with a plastic card programmed*

8Y *troublesome or non-paying hotel guests can be locked out of their rooms at the touch of a keyboard, and lost keys no longer represent a security risk. Great for the hotel management*

9N *The front door key has yet to be replaced by the plastic swipe card, and I doubt it will in the foreseeable future.*

11 6 Most new motor vehicles still do not have remote locks.

7 Hotel guests prefer plastic room keys to conventional ones.

8 Hotels fail to appreciate the benefits of computerised room keys.

9 It will be a long time before all dwellings are fitted with electronic keys.

Sentence completion with a box

12 B

13 A is ungrammatical; C is illogical.

14 B

15 F

16 A

17 D

Summary completion

18 Question 19 will be a singular noun; Question 20 will be a plural noun.

19 Noun / singular – could be a place

20 Noun / plural – something valuable from the past

21 Noun / plural – people, perhaps swimmers or divers

22 £10 million

23 failures / crashes

24 large

25 banking (systems)

26 disastrous

27 a programme   **d** critical networks

b finding ways to stop   **e** says

c are untestable

Summary completion with a box

28 important algae / expelled / occurs / turns

29 algae being expelled

30 coral bleaching

31 E

32 A

33 G

34 D

35 *some systems are now so large / they are untestable / scheme has been given added urgency / if a century-old technology like a power grid can fail*

General Training Writing Task 1

Content

1 Suggested answer:

B	No	Dear Sir/Madam Yours faithfully	No card in envelope	What if the card has gone to someone else?	Who will pay?	Looking forward to a prompt reply
C	Yes	Dear Leo Best wishes	Great to see each other after all this time	Particularly enjoyed the picnic	Must come to stay with me	Hope to hear from you soon

2 a sorry   **b** lent   **c** found

3 I'm writing to say that I'm sorry for not giving you back the book

4 a let   **e** post
   b need   **f** money
   c manage   **g** want
   d send

5 a I **b** I **c** F **d** F **e** I **f** I

6 a B **b** I **c** I **d** F **e** F **f** F **g** I **h** I **i** I **j** I **k** F **l** B

7 Letter B
Dear Sir, I recently received a letter from my bank which stated that my new bank card had been sent to me. However, the card was not enclosed in the envelope.

Letter C
Dear Leo, I'm writing to thank you for your great hospitality over the weekend. It was wonderful to see you again after all this time and it was terrific to get out of the city and breathe all that fresh air.

Organisation

1 a , which   **f** but obviously
   b Unfortunately,   **g** it
   c but   **h** because
   d even though   **i** Could you tell me
   e , which   **j** it

2 Suggested answer:
I'm writing to thank you for a really enjoyable visit. It was good to see you after so long, and to be able to spend some time with you, talking about old schoolfriends and teachers.
Now that I'm back home, I keep thinking about how good it was to be somewhere quiet and peaceful. I particularly enjoyed our trip to the wildlife sanctuary and appreciated the opportunity to see so many rare birds and animals. It's made me think that I should try and do more to protect them, so I'm having a look on the internet to see what sort of organisations there are.
Perhaps next time we get together you could come and visit me. There are plenty of places we could go and my brother would really like to meet you. Let me know when you might be free to come here and we can fix something up.
Look forward to hearing from you.

Vocabulary

1 a F **b** I **c** F **d** F **e** I
   a I'm writing to enquire
   b Lovely … Thanks … great
   c Thank you … I'd be grateful
   d I'd like to apologise … late arrival … due to
   e Great to catch up … Sorry … bit late

2 location / salary / hours / enquire / accommodation / live-in / restaurant / experience / porter / waiter / chambermaid / dealing with guests / weekend work / shifts / could you advise me / could you let me know / give me an idea

3 a accept / sincere
   b received / unexpected
   c had / appalling
   d made / serious
   e given / legal
   f showed / genuine
   g took / unforgettable
   h submitted / online

4 Simpson / apologise / Wednesday / missed / opportunity / sit or take / most of the / good / important / whenever / very much / hope

5 Suggested answer:
- explain why you were late
- request another chance to take the test
- reassure your tutor that you will work hard for it

Grammar

1 Suggested answer:
   a When emptying my suitcase, I found a book at the bottom of it.
   b Why not come and visit us if you have any free time next year?
   c The letter which you sent me arrived late and had no bank card in it.
   d I'm looking for a hotel job that involves some administration work.
   e Could you tell me whether you have any part-time jobs?
   f I need to request some time off to stay with my brother, whose wife is having a baby.

2 a am writing   **f** would
   b have   **g** will
   c would   **h** am
   d have   **i** can / will
   e is getting   **j** look forward

3 as a waiter / am looking for / quite a lot of / was working or worked / enjoyed it / interested / would prefer / how much you pay / I would appreciate hearing

General Training Writing Task 2

Content

1

B	Yes	ideal holiday / normal routine / stay at home / going away	One – the benefit of going away
C	Yes	films / DVD market / internet / affecting cinema audiences	Two – the positive and negative side of DVDs

2 There are two questions to address in C, so your position will relate both to the effect on audiences and to whether you think this is positive or negative.

3 Your own answer.

4 The final sentence represents position i.

5 Suggested answer:

In my view, it is just as relaxing to spend some time at home. It can be very stressful organising a holiday.

6 The writer's position is re-stated from *The enormous benefits*… onwards.

7 Suggested answer:

In the past, the simple act of 'going to the cinema' was as important as whether you enjoyed the film or not. Now, the fact that people can choose whether to go out to see a film or stay at home changes their attitude and, as a result, I believe the number of people going to the cinema is falling.

8 Suggested answer:

Positives	Negatives
Can choose from a wide range of films	Fewer big blockbusters will be produced
Can watch films at any time	Harder to control what children watch
Can download films from the internet	Encourages more passive viewing

9 The second sentence contains the supporting argument.

10 Suggested answer:

In many countries, it is a legal requirement that people working in dangerous jobs should wear safety equipment to minimise the risk of injuring themselves and reduce the likelihood of accidents. This is obviously a good idea, in principle, as it protects workers' health and increases the efficiency of the workforce. It also protects employers from insurance claims.

However, these laws can sometimes go too far, and the safety equipment can make it difficult to do the job properly. For example, wearing a mask to stop you breathing in dust or fumes sounds like a good idea, but after a short while it could become uncomfortable or cause other problems. So the laws may not always be helpful.

Organisation

1 The main ideas are the second and fourth sentences. The second paragraph should start: *How can parents control*… because this is the start of a new idea.

2 Another concern is how parents can…

3 1 the most important reason 2 also 3 however

4 Suggested answer:

Children, *in particular*, cannot make decisions about safety *because* they are too young, *so* laws are good in this case.

5

it	*the pool*	they	*young children*
it	*the pool*	these	*(the first sentence)*
This	*the high fence or barrier*	they	*regulations*

6 **a** one
b this / the
c who
d their
e these
f These
g their
h they
i one

7 but / and / another / and / although

8 Suggested answer:

In my country people who work on building sites are not well protected by the law and consequently there are many accidents every year, some of which are fatal. In my view, construction workers should be required to have a certain level of experience and should not be expected to work in bad weather or with sub-standard equipment. These simple guidelines would improve their working conditions considerably.

Vocabulary

1 It comes from a newspaper article.

2 **a** flights
b air traffic
c airports
d airlines / traveller(s)
e global warming
f noise pollution
g airline companies

3 **a** roughly
b quicker
c relaxing
d scenery
e unpleasant
f stressful
g flying
h particularly
i airlines
j flights

Grammar

1 **a** *don't*
b commas round *for example*
c comma after *you*
d comma after *Similarly*
e *it's*
f full stop after *nearby* and start new sentence
g comma after *calm*
h full stop at end

Speaking Part 1

1 a

2 Suggested answer:

a Canterbury.

b Canterbury's in the south-east corner of England. It's quite near the coast.

c I've lived there for 18 years.

d Yes, it's OK. It's quite a big city so there are plenty of things for young people to do, lots of shops and some parks. And it's a historical place so there are some very interesting tourist sites there.

e Not really. I suppose I'd quite like it if it was a bit bigger. But I think, on the whole, it's a good place to live.

3 Suggested answer:

What kind of work or studies do you do?

Where do you work or study?

How long have you had this job / been studying?

Do you like your area of work or study?

Is there anything you dislike about it?

4 Suggested answer:

Reading material: magazine/book/comic

Forms of transport: bus/motorbike/tram

Types of building: museum/factory/school

Weather: sunshine/mist/snow

Types of celebration: wedding/festival/party
Hobbies/interests: dancing/swimming/languages
Types of entertainment: film/tenpin bowling/karaoke
Types of scenery: moorland/desert/coastline

5 Your own answer.

6 a tiring
  b impressive
  c informative
  d depressing
  e enjoyable / relaxing / sociable
  f scary / impressive
  g sociable
  h relaxing
  i complicated / depressing

7 b flight
  c polluted
  d helpful
  e freedom
  f comfortable
  g golfer
  h crowded

8 a C **b** B **c** E **d** D **e** A **f** D **g** E

9 Suggested answer:
  B I prefer to travel by car because I like to look at the scenery. Although planes can get you there a lot quicker, I think I find air travel a bit stressful.
  C When I'm on holiday, I like to visit interesting places in the area. I'm an active person, so beach holidays and that kind of thing don't really interest me. I need to do things.
  D I think people have to have a break from their everyday routine so that they can feel refreshed. Also, these days, life has become extremely hectic. Everyone's always in a rush, so we need to slow things down from time to time.
  E For my last holiday, I went camping in the countryside with some friends. It was much better than I'd expected. The weather was really warm and we did lots of hill walking and got very fit. I didn't enjoy the food very much, though!

10 Suggested answer:
  a My favourite subject's English because it's very useful and…
  b At school. I started learning English when I was only five, so I've been doing it a long time!
  c I much prefer a small class. Big classes are far too impersonal and it's never possible for the teacher to give their attention to everyone.
  d Yes, I'm going to take IELTS because…
  e A school play! I can't really remember… maybe I was in one when I was very young.
  f Yes, they've introduced several changes. One is… another is…

11 a I come from Tokyo.
  b I play basketball.
  c Yes. I like fashion very much.
  d I have lived with my family since I was born.

e I find it hard to pronounce English words. / It isn't easy for me to pronounce English words.
  f I enjoy discussing economics.
  g I'm thinking of going to America.
  h Most people go away in the summer.
  i I don't eat much fruit.

Speaking Part 2

1 scientific development / benefited / what type / why needed / how used / why beneficial

2 Suggested answer:
  A winter sports / cross-country skiing
  B school trip / visit from relatives
  C singer / sportsperson
  D carnival / festival
  E weekend job / job for parents
  F school pantomime / music festival

3 Although getting married seemed an easy topic, it wasn't. The student decided on it before he had thought about whether he had enough things to say.

4 Your own answer.

5 The plan that you have more to say about produces more ideas in your notes.

6 enjoy / 've always been / was / used to watch / dream / had / were / have / try

7 Points: why you like it; when you started doing it; how often you do it now.

8 A was born / lived / finished or had finished / went / was
  B is / elected / stays / is or would be / would feel
  C got / was / came / don't / was

9 a hiking
  b schoolfriends
  c mountain
  d takes hours
  e steep
  f view from the top

Speaking Part 3

1 a, c, d, f, h

2 benefits / travelling / new places

3 The student could illustrate the key ideas (see below). By giving a full answer the student may also be able to influence the direction of the discussion.
  Sample answer:
  I think there are quite a number of benefits. For a start, it can be very exciting to visit a different country, *because you see and experience things that are quite new and unfamiliar to you*, and it can also be personally rewarding too. *For example, you might change your plans for the future as a result of your trip.*

4 Your own answer.

5 countries rely on tourism

6 Job / work / career / choosing a career / value of work / employer's responsibilities

Fun in preparing for the performance / benefits of taking part / using drama in school education / value of the theatre and cinema in society

7 How would you advise people to choose a career?
How important is work in a person's life?
Is it right that a nurse gets less money than a doctor?
What might you learn from taking part in a performance?
Should children have the chance to perform at school?
What role do the arts play in society today?

8 Suggested answer:

For me having a hobby is terribly important *because* I get very stressed in my job, so I have to do something that relaxes me. If I didn't have any hobbies, I think I would just work and that would be very bad for my health.

Some people feel that sport is a waste of time because there are so many other things to do in life. Perhaps if they're really busy, they have a point. *But I actually think* you learn a lot of social skills through sport, like working as part of a team and negotiating tactics.

I don't really think the Olympic Games are a very good way of building international relations. I think people get too serious about their own country winning. *On the other hand, the FIFA World Cup is always fantastic. I really* think it unites everyone who enjoys it – we're all watching it at the same time and we get involved in games even if our own country isn't playing.

Practice Test

Listening Section 1

1 to **3** D, E, H (in any order)
4 29 LOCH Street
5 558 992
6 Saturday 1 May / 1st May / May 1st
7 8 weeks / 2 months
8 A
9 E
10 D

Listening Section 2

11 cities
12 (a) palace
13 (the) coat hanger
14 government / state / state government
15 1924
16 800 houses
17 9.5 million
18 horse
19 2.3 kms / 2.3 kilometres
20 (a) ship / (an) earthquake

Listening Section 3

21 A
22 H
23 D
24 E
25 A
26 (the) Painted Gallery
27 (the) Main Gallery
28 B
29 A
30 C

Listening Section 4

31 selling / advertising (must have both words)
32 making money / profit
33 warmth / safety (must have both words)
34 individual
35 C **36** A **37** B **38** A
39 satisfied
40 better than expected

General Training Reading Section 1

1 48
2 11
3 19
4 36
5 42
6 T
7 F
8 NG
9 F
10 F
11 warm clothes
12 women's aerobics
13 1.00 pm / 1 pm
14 (own) mat

General Training Reading Section 2

15 iv
16 ii
17 i
18 vii
19 v
20 vi
21 B
22 C
23 E
24 A
25 D
26 B
27 C

General Training Reading Section 3

28 Y
29 N
30 NG
31 N
32 Y
33 C
34 G
35 B
36 D
37 F
38 instrument
39 sampling
40 triumph

General Training Writing Task 1

Suggested answer:

Dear Robert,

Hi there. I hope you're enjoying your college year. Thanks very much for asking me to come and visit you in Singapore. As you know, I haven't travelled to Asia before, so I thought I'd write and ask you a few questions.

I want to bring a present with me and I wondered what would be appropriate. Perhaps you could let me know what your mum's hobbies are and then I could come up with an idea based on one of them.

Also, what sort of clothes should I bring? I know it's pretty warm where you live but do I need jumpers or a coat? What sort of activities are we likely to do while I'm there and should I bring things like swimming gear or trainers?

Lastly, I hate to be a nuisance but I hope you remember that I'm a vegetarian. I do eat fish and eggs but I don't eat red meat or chicken at all. Is that going to be a problem?

Look forward to hearing from you.

Barnaby

Style:	Informal because it is to a friend.
Beginning and ending:	Appropriately informal.
Purpose:	Last sentence of first paragraph.
Main ideas:	First sentence of each paragraph.
Paragraph breaks:	Each paragraph begins with a main idea and develops this.
Linkers:	as you know, so, and, also, but, lastly
Reference words:	one of them, where you live, there, that
Topic vocabulary:	travelled / Asia / present / appropriate / hobbies / pretty warm / jumpers / coat / activities / swimming gear / trainers / nuisance / vegetarian / fish / eggs / red meat / chicken / problem
Less common vocabulary:	come up with, likely to do, hate to be a nuisance
Structures:	A range of verb phrases, tenses and complex sentences is used.
Length:	176 words

General Training Writing Task 2

Suggested answer:

It is generally accepted that we all need leisure time to recover from the stresses of work and everyday life. Personally, I prefer to be active during this time, as I think this suits me better. However, what we do with our leisure time is up to us and no one can say that any particular activity is the best.

Some people relax by watching movies, reading or surfing the internet. People who have physically demanding jobs may choose these types of activities. If you are a nurse or builder, you may feel that you don't want to do a five-kilometre run after work, because you are already physically tired.

Other people do very sedentary jobs. Computer analysts, for example, may spend all day sitting in front of a computer screen. At the end of the working day, they may be keen to stretch their limbs and improve their health by swimming or going to the gym.

Another factor that influences our choice of leisure pursuit is where we work. People who work indoors often prefer outdoor hobbies, whereas for people who work outdoors, the reverse may be true. I am a student myself and this involves a lot of sitting in lectures, so I need to get out into the fresh air afterwards.

In any situation, the important thing is that people need to stay healthy by choosing what is best for them. The only wrong way to spend free time, in my view, is to have a sedentary job and then go home and watch television.

Position:	The writer personally prefers to be active but says there is no right answer.
Main ideas:	First two sentences of second paragraph; first and last sentences of third paragraph; first sentence of fourth paragraph.
Linkers:	as, however, some people, if, other people, for example, another factor, whereas, so, in any situation, and then
References:	this time, this, these types of activities, their limbs, the reverse, this
Topic vocabulary:	leisure time / stresses of work / everyday life / active / activity / relax / watching movies / reading / surfing the internet / physically demanding jobs / run / tired / sedentary / working day / stretch limbs / swimming / going to the gym / leisure pursuit / work indoors / outdoor hobbies / sitting / fresh air / stay healthy / spend free time / job / watch television
Sentence types:	A range of complex sentence types is used.

Speaking Part 1

The student gave relevant answers to all the questions, using a range of appropriate vocabulary and linkers. The answers were clear and sufficiently long for Part 1.

Speaking Part 2

The student was able to speak for two minutes and kept to the topic. He covered all the points in the task and used a range of vocabulary and linkers. He allowed himself time to think, when necessary.

Speaking Part 3

The student responded well to the main ideas in the questions and gave full answers, with plenty of support. He discussed the topics with ease, using a good range of words and expressions. As the student was a native speaker, he made no grammatical errors, pronounced words clearly and used rhythm, stress and intonation well.

Recording Scripts

Listening Section 1

Extract 1 (CD Track 1)

Man   Good morning. Motor Registry.

Woman   Oh, good morning. I'd like to arrange a day to take my driving test.

Man   OK. Have you done the Knowledge Test yet?

Woman   Yes, I've passed that. I got 99%.

Man   Right. What's your name and I'll just check that on the computer. Oh, no! The computers aren't working right now. You'll have to give me your details and I'll call you back. What's your name?

Woman   Caroline Black, that's C A R O L I N E Black.

Man   OK and your date of birth?

Woman   22nd of November, 1984.

Man   November the 22nd, that's today. Happy birthday! Nineteen eighty-four. And can you give me a contact number so I can call you back?

Woman   I'll give you my mobile – it's 0412 129 807.

Man   0412 129... Did you say 811?

Woman   No... 807.

Man   Right. Got it. And can you tell me what make and model of car you'll be using for the test?

Woman   Yes, it's a Ford – a Ford station wagon. It's my dad's car.

Man   OK. Ford station wagon. Well, when the computers are working again, I'll call you back with a date for the test.

Woman   Oh. All right. Thanks...

Extract 2 (CD Track 2)

Woman   Excuse me. Can you tell me how to get to the library? I seem to have got rather lost.

Man   Sure! Well you're a little off course. It's about a ten-minute walk from here. Have you got a map?

Woman   Yes. Here it is.

Man   Now, let me see. You're here at the moment. I'll put a cross on the map to show you where you are.

Woman   Thanks.

Man   OK. So you walk along George Street, past the Queen Victoria Building on your left. We call that the QVB.

Woman   Oh, I see.

Man   Go past the QVB and turn right into Market Street. There's a bank on the opposite corner. And a department store on the other corner.

Woman   So I turn right.

Man   Yes, you turn right and walk past a lovely old theatre on your right, that's opposite the department store. That's called the State Theatre.

Woman   OK. Past the theatre and...

Man   Then you need to turn left into Pitt Street. That's a pedestrian street, with no cars and lots of shops. There are shops along both sides of the street.

Woman   Oh, yes, I think I've been there before.

Man   Walk along Pitt Street until you come to Martin Place. The old post office building is on your left – except that it's not the post office any more, it's now a big hotel; the post office has gone.

Woman   Oh that's a shame. I bet it's an expensive hotel!

Man   Probably. I've never stayed there myself! Go across Martin Place, and then just continue walking along Pitt Street and you'll come to Hunter Street. Turn right and then walk straight ahead for a couple of blocks until you come to a main road. The library is on the other side of the road, but you can't miss it.

Woman   Thank you so much.

Listening Section 2

Extract 1 (CD Track 3)

On today's programme about great buildings of the world, I'm going to talk about the Bell Rock lighthouse – perhaps one of the greatest engineering feats of the 19th century, and I'm sure you'll agree that this is a fascinating story. It's nearly 200 years since the lighthouse was first built, and when you look at where it's situated, you'll see why this was such a remarkable achievement.

The Bell Rock lighthouse, also known as Stevenson's lighthouse after the engineer who built it, is 11 miles off the east coast of Scotland in the North Sea. It consists of a white stone tower over 100 feet high, that's over 30 metres high, and it rises out of the sea, apparently without any support. It is a truly amazing sight! But, in fact, despite what it looks like, the tower is actually built on a sandstone reef which lies just under the waves.

Because the Bell Rock is underwater for so much of the time, it has always presented a great danger to shipping and many ships were lost over the centuries. And, it has also presented a huge engineering challenge, for it's no easy business to build a lighthouse under such conditions. In the first year of construction, work could only take place in the summer months when the tide was low. And it is a credit to Stevenson and his colleagues that this incredible structure has not required a single repair to its stonework since the day it was completed in 1811...

Extract 2 (CD Track 4)

Thank you for calling the Rialto Family Cinemas. The following information is for Saturday 3rd February. Please collect reserved tickets 15 minutes before the commencement of the film. In Cinema One, we are showing *Shrek 2*, the sequel to the smash hit *Shrek*. One performance only this morning at a quarter past eleven. This is an animated fairytale – suitable for all the family.

In Cinema Two, we have the award-winning documentary *The Long Journey* commencing at 6.15 pm. Don't miss this extraordinary first-hand account.

In Cinema Three, by popular demand, the Jackie Chan favourite *Armour of God*. Commencing at 5.30 pm with a repeat performance at 9.15. This is Jackie Chan at his best in a classic action film.

Extract 3 (CD Track 5)

Welcome to the City Art Gallery and to our gallery audio tour. The Gallery was first established in 1875 and is now one of the city's most popular attractions. The building has undergone a number of changes over the years, the most recent addition being the extension on the ground floor, which was opened in 1988.

The Gallery houses some of the finest works of art in Australia including Aboriginal, European and Asian paintings. There is a comprehensive Australian collection, which includes works from the early colonial period to the present day. In addition to the paintings on display, we have an excellent collection of photography, with photographs dating from the 19th century.

As well as the permanent collection which you will see throughout the building, the Art Gallery has a varied and exciting exhibition programme with approximately 30 changing exhibitions each year. Many of these exhibitions are accompanied by films and lectures or occasionally by concerts.

Now let's begin our tour in the 19th century Australian room…

Listening Section 3

Extract 1 (CD Track 6)

Man So flamingos in zoos need to eat algae, do they? Why's that?

Woman Well, for a long while, flamingos living in captivity, for example in zoos, kept losing their delicate pink colour and fading to white. Then the zookeepers realised the problem was due to the birds' diet.

Man Weren't they getting enough food?

Woman No, that wasn't the problem. It was that, in the wild, flamingos feed on a certain kind of algae containing chemicals called carotenoids, which give the birds their distinctive colour.

Extract 2 (CD Track 7)

Man I believe researchers are exploring the idea of a padded car to reduce injuries in accidents. Can you tell us something about what it will be like?

Woman Yes. Well, the car will be covered in plastic cells filled with air, moulded round a conventional metal frame.

Man I see. So the plastic cells will allow cars to bounce off each other.

Woman Exactly. And you'd also be able to see what's just behind you on the road because there's a camera mounted on the back.

Man Any other innovations?

Woman The doors will open upwards and out, giving the appearance of a wing when open, and the wheels will go in all directions to assist in heavy traffic. And to guide motorists away from traffic jams and help them find a parking spot, the car will be fitted with a computer near the steering wheel.

Man Where the driver can see it, of course.

Woman Yes. There's also a hook to allow novel parking techniques.

Man It sounds amazing!

Listening Section 4

Extract 1 (CD Track 8)

Did you know that within the nucleus of each of your cells is a set of instructions for building you from scratch? Amazingly, if you could stretch it out, this string of acid, or DNA as it is known, would be about three feet long: but in fact, it's tangled up like a ball of string. Various parts of the string incorporate between 50,000 and 100,000 separate genes. A human individual's complete set of genetic material is known as the human genome. And interestingly, the human genome is not the biggest one around. Surprisingly enough, your genome has a lot in common with other animals and plants. Nonetheless, your DNA sequence is uniquely yours.

Extract 2 (CD Track 9)

Lonely Planet is one of a number of highly successful publishers of travel books. The company is based in Australia but also has offices in a number of other countries. The travel guide business is a highly competitive market, and so to compete, they have adopted a range of marketing strategies. One thing they excel at is tracking individual customers, which in turn allows them to measure how well their marketing is working. They've also licensed the name, Lonely Planet, to a TV programme of the same name, as part of their overall strategy.

Extract 3 (CD Track 10)

The production of olive oil is an expensive business. The best oil comes from olives that have been hand picked, as machines tend to damage the fruit, so the first step is to pick the olives by hand. After this initial process, the fruit is transported to the mills, where it is carefully crushed. Incidentally the very best oil, known as extra virgin oil, comes from the first crush. The paste which results from the crushing process is mixed until oil droplets form and the precious 'liquid gold' is then bottled in beautiful containers and labelled to show its origin. The oil finally finds its way into shops and supermarkets both at home and abroad.

Extract 4 (CD Track 11)

Some people believe that when you're learning a language, the best way to improve your speaking is in the language laboratory, but I firmly believe that it's better to work in small groups because then you can also improve your listening at the same time. After all, speaking and listening go together, don't they? And somehow it seems more natural to work in groups. The language lab is a good enough place to practise your pronunciation and you can also improve your grammar by doing practice drills in the lab, even if it's a bit boring. As far as reading is concerned, nothing beats working on your own and reading as much as possible whenever you have the chance.

Practice Test Recording Scripts

Section 1 (CD Track 12)

Agent Good morning. Can I help you?

Customer Yes, I'd like to get some information about trips to New Zealand.

Agent Certainly. Take a seat and I'll be right with you.

Customer Thanks.

Agent	Now, where would you like to go in New Zealand?
Customer	Well, I was hoping to do a bit of travelling around, actually. There are a few things I'd like to see and do before I go back home.
Agent	Right.
Customer	One thing I really want to do is go to Christchurch. I <u>have relatives living there that I can stay with</u> – my mother's cousin – and I've heard it's a nice place.
Agent	Yes, it's a lovely city. And staying with relatives will help with the budget, of course.
Customer	The budget?
Agent	It will save you some money.
Customer	Oh right! Well, I'm not too worried about that. I've saved quite a bit of money working in Australia.
Agent	Oh, that's nice. Good for you! Well, you know that New Zealand consists of two main islands, the North Island and the South Island, and Christchurch is on the South Island.
Customer	Is it? I was never very good at geography at school! Do you have a map I could look at?
Agent	Sure! Here we are.
Customer	Right. I see. And… well… then I'd also like to spend some time in Auckland. <u>And maybe I could do an English language course there.</u> Can you organise that sort of thing for me?
Agent	Certainly. We'd be happy to arrange that. But bear in mind that Auckland is in the North Island.
Customer	OK. And I'd also like to do some <u>skiing or maybe even some snowboarding.</u> I hear New Zealand is a great place for that.
Agent	Yes, absolutely. But you should go to Auckland first for your studies, and then you can get the ferry across to the South Island and take the bus down to the snow.
Customer	Oh, I don't like boats very much. I'm not much of a sailor. I think I'd prefer to fly.
Agent	Right. What about joining a walking tour? That could be really fun.
Customer	Not sure about walking, but joining a tour might be a good way to travel, because then I might <u>make some friends my own age.</u>
Pause	
Agent	Now, let's get some details. Can I have your name, please.
Customer	Yes, it's Su Ming Lee, but you can call me Sue.
Agent	OK, Sue. And what's your address here in Melbourne?
Customer	I'm living with my aunt in the suburb of Kew. <u>It's 29 Loch Street. That's L O C H not L O C K.</u>
Agent	Do you have a phone number that I can get you on?
Customer	The best thing would be if I give you my mobile. I always have it on me. It's <u>0 4 0 2 double 5 8 double 9 2.</u>
Agent	OK. And when do you want to travel? Because you'll need to be down south in July or August.
Customer	Oh, yes. Of course. That's winter, isn't it? So I'd better go to Auckland in May…

Agent	Yes. Let's say <u>departing from Melbourne on the first of May – that's a Saturday</u> – and then you could begin your course on Monday the third.
Customer	That sounds great!
Agent	And how long would you like to study for? A month, two, three? What do you think?
Customer	Well, I'll probably need more than a month. <u>What about eight weeks… until the end of June.</u>
Agent	Fine. I'll see what I can do. Oh, and how would you like to pay for this?
Customer	On my Visa card if that's possible.
Pause	
Agent	Hello Sue. It's Angelo from Kosmos Travel here. I've booked your flight and I've found you an English college called The Harbour Language Centre.
Customer	Great! Where exactly is that?
Agent	Well, have you got that little map I gave you yesterday?
Customer	Yes.
Agent	You see where the harbour is, with the three wharves and the water?
Customer	Yes, got that.
Agent	OK, there are two parallel streets – Quay Street, that's Q U A Y and Customs Street. The building where the college is located is <u>on Quay Street, opposite Princes Wharf.</u>
Customer	Right, got it. And what about accommodation?
Agent	Well, I've booked you into a hotel for the first three nights and then the accommodation officer will find you a family to live with.
Customer	Good. And where's the hotel?
Agent	It's a short walk from the college, <u>on the corner of Queen Street and City Road.</u>
Customer	Which corner exactly?
Agent	On the <u>left-hand side</u> as we are looking at the map.
Customer	OK. Near the little park.
Agent	Yes, that's right.
Customer	And what about a good bookshop? I'm going to need to buy a dictionary and some English books.
Agent	Yes. Well, I believe there's a really good language bookshop on the <u>corner of Customs Street and Queen Street.</u> It's near the college so that's pretty convenient.
Customer	Thank you so much. You've been really helpful.

Section 2 (CD Track 13)

Announcer

The Sydney Harbour Bridge is nearly three-quarters of a century old and, to help celebrate this important occasion, our reporter Sarah Chambers has compiled this brief history of her favourite bridge.

Sarah

A bridge is more than just a crossing over a river or a waterway – it is a landmark in its own right; a landmark which allows us to identify one <u>city</u> from another. Think, for instance, of the Bridge of Sighs in Venice, or the magnificent Charles Bridge in Prague. Each of <u>these cities can be recognised by their famous bridges.</u> The Golden Gate Bridge in San Francisco is another example of a city known by its bridge. But in addition to this, a bridge is a kind of ornament for a city, similar, if you like, to a cathedral or a palace.

Here in Sydney we may not have our own palace, but we do have our famous and much loved bridge – The Sydney Harbour Bridge, which is sometimes affectionately known as 'the coat hanger' because of its arched shape. It was built back in the 1930s, and so the bridge is coming up for a significant birthday. Let's have a little look at its history.

Pause

Although the idea of building a crossing over Sydney harbour had been discussed many years earlier, it wasn't until the year 1916 that the state government agreed to allocate some money for the construction of a bridge.

The chief engineer for the bridge was a man called Dr John Bradfield, a brilliant engineer who supervised the entire project from beginning to end. First they had to decide on a design, so he organised an international competition to choose a design, and ultimately got the one he wanted. The job went to a British engineering firm and the contract was signed in 1924. The design he chose was the single-arch bridge that you see today, made of steel, with a tower at either end.

In 1926, construction finally began. The first thing they had to do was demolish 800 houses around the site where the towers were to be built. The poor families, however, never received any compensation for this! But the project created thousands of jobs – much needed in those difficult times. Of course, like all projects of this size, it took much longer to build than originally planned – it was supposed to have been finished by 1930 – but actually it wasn't completed for another two years. It also cost twice as much as the original quote, coming in at £9.5 million instead of the agreed contract price of £4.2 million! But what's new?

The opening ceremony took place on 19 March 1932, and a large crowd gathered for the occasion. The Premier of the State was just about to cut the ribbon when suddenly a man rode through the crowd mounted on a horse and slashed the ribbon with his sword. He wanted to be the first to cut the ribbon. Anyway, they tied the ribbon back together and the ceremony continued. The man on the horse was fined £5 for his offensive behaviour!

Since then, millions of cars have crossed the bridge, each paying a toll to do so. By the early 1980s the government had paid off the loan for the money they'd borrowed all those years before, but motorists continued to pay to cross from north to south. This money was subsequently used to build a tunnel under the harbour to reduce the amount of traffic on the bridge.

Pause

The tunnel was opened in 1992 and cost $544 million. It is 2·3 kilometres long and is equipped with all the latest technology, including closed circuit television to monitor any problems. And it has most definitely reduced the load on the bridge, as it carries around 75,000 vehicles each day which would otherwise have to use the bridge. And it's apparently strong enough to withstand the impact of a ship or even the impact of an earthquake.

The tunnel has been a welcome solution to Sydney's traffic problems, but, of course, a tunnel could never compete with a bridge as a landmark for any city. So let's wish the bridge a very happy birthday!

Section 3 (CD Track 14)

Mia	Hello, David.
David	Oh hi, Mia. Sorry I'm a bit late.
Mia	Oh. No problem! Thanks for agreeing to help me with my assignment today. I really needed to go over it with someone.
David	Sure. You were going to talk about European rock art, weren't you?
Mia	Yes, the rock drawings in the caves of Lascaux in western France.
David	Oh, fantastic, over 13,000 years old, I believe. What sort of drawings are they?
Mia	They're drawings of animals on the whole, but you can also find some human representations, as well as some signs. There are roughly 600 drawings at Lascaux.
David	Really? Were they mostly pictures of bulls?
Mia	Well, no, actually, the animal most depicted was the horse. Have a look at this graph. It shows the distribution of the different animals. You see… first the horse, and then after that a sort of prehistoric bull…
David	Oh, OK. That's interesting, isn't it?
Mia	…and the third most commonly drawn creature was the stag. There were some other animals but these are the main ones.
David	What are the drawings like? I mean, what sort of style?
Mia	Well, the bulls are depicted very figuratively – they're not very realistic. They are very big by comparison to the other drawings, of people and signs. They appear to be almost three-dimensional in some cases, following the contours of the cave walls, but of course they're not.
David	Amazing. Perhaps they felt these animals were the most impressive and needed to be represented like that.
Mia	Yeah, maybe. The drawings of humans by contrast consist of just simple lines. Like the stick figures my little sister draws. Perhaps humans were seen as less important.
David	Mmm, perhaps. What about the signs. How did they draw them?
Mia	There doesn't appear to be much evidence of signs, and those that have been found are usually made up of little points.
David	Rather like Aboriginal art from Australia.
Mia	Yes. Something like that, but not as complex, of course.
David	So apart from the bulls and horses and stags, were there any other creatures depicted?
Mia	In one or two chambers, you do find pictures of fish but they're quite rare.

Pause

David	What sort of size is the cave? It must be quite large to have that many pictures.
Mia	Well, it's actually a number of inter-linking chambers, really. Here's a map showing where the different drawings can be found.
David	Oh, good. Let's have a look at that.
Mia	The first 20 metres inside the cave slope down very steeply to the first hall in the network. That's called the Great Hall of the Bulls.
David	Here. OK.
Mia	Then off to the left we have the Painted Gallery, which is about 30 metres long, and is basically a continuation of this first hall.
David	But further into the cave.
Mia	Exactly. Then we find a second, lower gallery called the Lateral Passage. This opens off the aisle to the right of the Great Hall of the Bulls. It connects the next chamber with an area known as the Main Gallery. At the end of the Main Gallery is the Chamber of Felines. There are one or two other connecting chambers but there's no evidence of man having been in these rooms.
Pause	
David	Is the cave open to the public today?
Mia	Well, no. Because after the initial discovery in 1940, it was opened and literally millions of people came through to see the drawings. Then in the fifties the experts started to worry about the damage being done to the drawings, and the government finally closed the Lascaux cave in 1963.
David	Is that so!
Mia	It wasn't really the tourists that were doing the harm, but the fact that after thousands of years, the cave was suddenly open to the atmosphere and so bacteria and fungi started to destroy the pictures. You need a special permit to enter the cave now and very few people can get that unless they're scientists or have some official status.
David	It's a shame, but I can see that they had to do something to protect the cave. So that means you can no longer see this rock art.
Mia	Well, not exactly. What they've done is re-create the drawings in a man-made cave, which you can visit.
David	Oh brilliant!
Mia	Yeah, the authorities decided to reproduce the two best sections of the site so they've created a life-size copy of the Hall of the Bulls and of the Painted Gallery. It's just a cement shell, which corresponds in shape to the interior of the original.
David	So now you can visit the caves without actually harming any of the 13,000-year-old paintings.

Section 4 (CD Track 15)

Last week we looked at some general principles associated with marketing and today I'd like to look at some of those points in a little more detail.

So what is marketing? Or put another way, what does the term 'marketing' mean? Many people think of it simply as the process of selling and advertising. And this is hardly surprising when every day we are bombarded with television adverts, mail shots, and telephone sales. But selling and advertising are only two functions of marketing.

In fact, marketing, more than any other business function, deals with customers. So perhaps the simplest definition is this one: marketing is the delivery of customer value and satisfaction at a profit. In other words, finding customers, keeping those customers happy and making money out of the process!

The most basic concept underlying marketing is the concept of human needs. These include basic physical needs for things like food, as well as warmth and safety. And marketers don't invent these needs; they're a basic part of our human make-up. So besides physical needs, there are also social needs – for instance, the need to belong and to be wanted. And in addition to social needs, we have the need for knowledge and self-expression, often referred to as individual needs.

As societies evolve, members of that society start to see things not so much in terms of what they need, but in terms of what they want, and when people have enough money these wants become demands.

Now, it's important for the managers in a company to understand what their customers want if they are going to create effective marketing strategies, so there are various ways of doing this. One way at supermarkets, for instance, is to interview customers while they're doing their shopping. They can be asked about their buying preferences and then the results of the survey can be analysed. This provides reliable feedback on which to base future marketing strategies. It's also quite normal for top executives from department stores to spend a day or two each month visiting stores and mixing freely with the public, as if they were ordinary customers, to get an idea of customer behaviour.

Another way to get information from customers is to give them something. For instance, some fast-food outlets give away vouchers in magazines or on the street that entitle customers to get part of their meal for nothing. As well as being a good way of attracting customers into the restaurants to spend their money, it also allows the managers to get a feel for where to advertise and which age-groups to target.

Another strategy employed at some well-known theme parks such as Disneyland is for top managers to spend at least one day in their career, touring the park dressed as Mickey Mouse or some other cartoon character. This provides them with the perfect opportunity to survey the scene and watch the customers without being noticed.

OK, well we mentioned customer satisfaction at the beginning of this lecture, and I'd like to return briefly to that, as it relates to what we've just been talking about. If the performance of a product falls short of the customer's expectations, the buyer is going to be dissatisfied. In other words, if the product you buy isn't as good as you'd expected, then the chances are you'll be unhappy about it. If, on the other hand, performance matches expectations, and the product you buy is as good as you expected, then generally speaking the buyer is satisfied. But smart companies should aim one step higher. They should aim to delight customers by promising only what they can be sure of delivering, and then delivering much more than they promised. So then, if as sometimes happens, performance is better than expected, the buyer is delighted and is twice as likely to come back to the store.

Now let's move on to look at the role of advertising…

Sample Answer Sheets

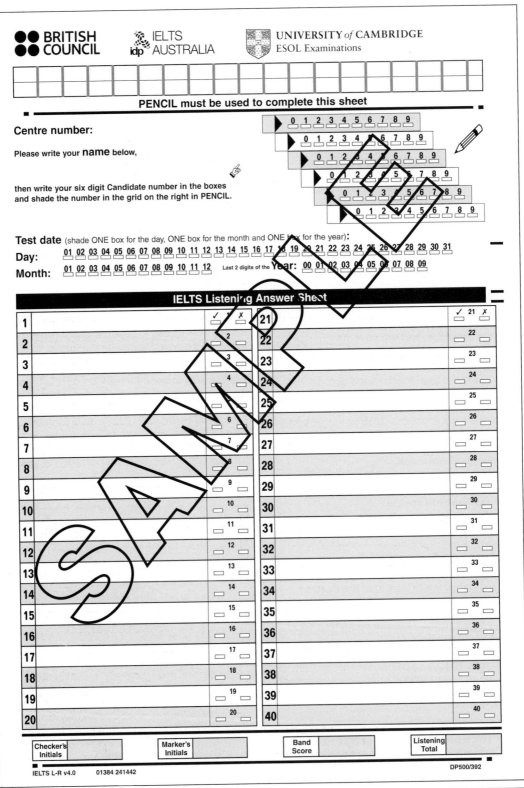

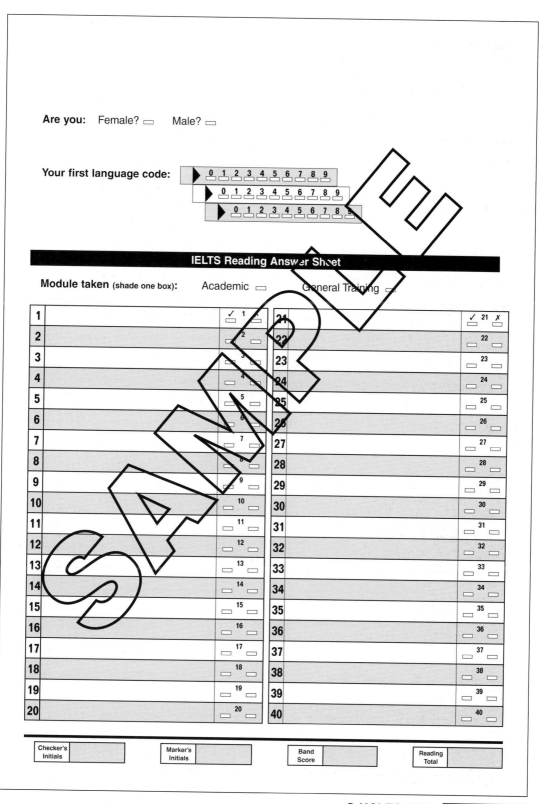

Are you: Female? ▭ Male? ▭

Your first language code: ▶ 0 1 2 3 4 5 6 7 8 9
▶ 0 1 2 3 4 5 6 7 8 9
▶ 0 1 2 3 4 5 6 7 8 9

IELTS Reading Answer Sheet

Module taken (shade one box):   Academic ▭   General Training ▭

1	✓ 1	21	✓ 21 ✗
2	2	22	22
3	3	23	23
4	4	24	24
5	5	25	25
6	6	26	26
7	7	27	27
8	8	28	28
9	9	29	29
10	10	30	30
11	11	31	31
12	12	32	32
13	13	33	33
14	14	34	34
15	15	35	35
16	16	36	36
17	17	37	37
18	18	38	38
19	19	39	39
20	20	40	40

| Checker's Initials | | Marker's Initials | | Band Score | | Reading Total | |

Acknowledgements

The authors and publishers would like to thank the teachers who commented on the material:

Australia: Garry Adams, Peter Gray; Brunei: Caroline Brandt; China: Gang He, Tao Sun, Chenggang Zhou; Japan: Alex Case; New Zealand: Belinda Hayes; Singapore: Jackie Williams; Spain: Chris Turner; Taiwan: Daniel Sansoni; UK: Frances Hughes, Diane Reeves, Karen Saxby, Roger Scott, Clare West, Norman Whitby.

The authors and publishers are grateful to the following for permission to use copyright material in *Action Plan for IELTS*. While every effort has been made, it has not been possible to identify the sources of all the material used and in such cases the publishers would welcome information from the copyright owners:

p. 24: illustration 'Prototype for a plastic car' and for the adapted text for the listening extract 2 (CD track 7) by Daniel Dasey and Colin Hamilton. Copyright © The *Sun-Herald*, August 2004; p. 35: text 'Hove Library' taken from the website www.citylibraries.info/libraries/hove.asp. Reproduced by permission of Brighton & Hove City Council; p. 36: extract 'The four-minute mile' from Greatest Event in World Sport by Simon Hollingsworth, published in *The Australian* May 2004. Reproduced by permission of Simon Hollingsworth; p. 37: extract 'Protecting you from card crime' taken from the Barclays Bank website. Reproduced by permission of Barclays Bank PLC; p. 39: extract 'Australian Visa Application', p. 92: extract 'Living in Australia', p. 93: 'Looking for Work', all taken from the website www.immi.gov.au. Inclusion of this material from the Australian Department of Immigration and Multicultural and Indigenous Affairs should in no way be interpreted as endorsement of this product. Copyright © Commonwealth of Australia 2005; p. 54: extract 'Sprawling systems on the edge of IT chaos' by Duncan Graham-Rowe *New Scientist* November 2004; p. 95: Information on Oxford Tutorial College taken from the website www.oxtutor.co.uk/retake/subjects/2004/film.htm. Copyright © Oxford Tutorial College 2005. Reproduced by permission of Oxford Tutorial College; p. 97: 'Mary had a little gramophone' by Jon Casimir published in *Sydney Morning Herald* November 1999. By kind permission of Jon Casimir.

The publishers are grateful to the following for permission to reproduce copyright photographs and material:

p. 6 (top): Andrew Bannister Gallo Images/CORBIS; pp. 6 (bottom), 30, 56, 74, 76, 80, 84: Paul Mulcahy; p. 16: www.fotoflite.com

Photo research by Val Mulcahy.

The recordings which accompany this book were made at Studio AVP, London.